LOS ANGELES
MAFIA CRIME FAMILY

A Complete History of a California

Criminal Organization

MAFIA LIBRARY

© **Copyright 2023 - All rights reserved.**

The content contained within this book may not be reproduced, duplicated or transmitted without direct written permission from the author or the publisher.

Under no circumstances will any blame or legal responsibility be held against the publisher, or author, for any damages, reparation, or monetary loss due to the information contained within this book, either directly or indirectly.

Legal Notice:

This book is copyright protected. It is only for personal use. You cannot amend, distribute, sell, use, quote or paraphrase any part, or the content within this book, without the consent of the author or publisher.

Disclaimer Notice:

Please note the information contained within this document is for educational and entertainment purposes only. All effort has been executed to present accurate, up to date, reliable, complete information. No warranties of any kind are declared or implied. Readers acknowledge that the author is not engaged in the rendering of legal, financial, medical or professional advice. The content within this book has been derived from various sources. Please consult a licensed professional before attempting any techniques outlined in this book.

By reading this document, the reader agrees that under no circumstances is the author responsible for any losses, direct or indirect, that are incurred as a result of the use of the information contained within this document, including, but not limited to, errors, omissions, or inaccuracies.

TABLE OF CONTENTS

Introduction 1
    Anatomy Of A Mafia 2
    The Roots Of The Sicilian Mafia 10
    The Rise Of The Mafias In Italy 11
    Expanding To The United States 13

Chapter 1 : Prohibition And The Founding Of The Los Angeles Crime Family 15
    Bootlegging And The Prohibition 15
    The Founding Of The Los Angeles Crime Family 21
    Joseph Ardizzone Mysteriously Vanishes 27

Chapter 2 : The Jack Dragna Era 29
    The Los Angeles Crime Family's New Boss 29
    Chief Sources Of Income 32
    Uneasy Relations 34
    The Battle Of Sunset Strip 41
    Lasting Legacy 45

Chapter 3 : Frank Desimone Takes Over 49
    A Decline In The Los Angeles Family 49
    Frank Desimone 51
    Ruining Reputations 52

Plotting The Death Of Desimone 53

Chapter 4 : Nicolo Licata's Rise To Power 55

Old Man Nick Licata 55

Licata Is Called To The Grand Jury 60

Licata's Life And Death 61

Chapter 5 : The Brooklier Decade 63

Reigning Brooklier 63

Death Ordered To Frank Bompensiero 65

Love-Hate Relationship 69

Another Hit To The Los Angeles Family 71

Later Charges And Imprisonment 72

Chapter 6 : The Milano Brothers 75

Peter And Carmen Milano 75

New Members Inducted 79

1984 Arrest 79

Chapter 7 : The Family Today 83

The Rise And Fall Of The Los Angeles Mafia 83

The Los Angeles Crime Family Today 88

Conclusion 93

References 97

INTRODUCTION

When you think of the Mafia and its headquarters, what city in the United States comes to mind? Most think of the Mafia organizations residing in and battling it out for power and money in Chicago, Detroit, and New York. However, even the glitz and glamor of Los Angeles has some darkness, as it was home to the Los Angeles Mafia crime family.

Mafias may be glorified in film, like in *The Godfather (1972)*; however, there is significantly more darkness in real life than we see on the screen. These organizations were socially accepted as they worked outside the law and were undoubtedly feared in the cities and neighborhoods where they lived. Their control stretched far and wide, from street-corner drugs to higher-ups in the government.

Over the years, the Mafia has controlled many different industries. One of the primary ones, often referenced in TV's hit show *The Sopranos*, is waste management. Because trash haulers are able to divvy up the areas they serve and sell routes to one another, it leaves significant room for the Mafia to move in with its strong-arm tactics. While Mayor Rudy Giuliani made it a top priority to tamp down on the Mafia activity within New York City during the 1990s, the crime families persisted.

The families have also been well-known throughout the years for their hold on the gambling industry. Of course, they have faced their fair share of indictments, arrests, and sentencings for illegal gambling activities. European countries have also raised concerns about the crime families using gambling websites to launder the money they earn. Other areas they have controlled over the decades include the pornography industry, real estate, construction, music recording, bars, restaurants, and drugs.

In their own way, Mafias are chosen families. Unlike a traditional family, crime and secrecy are at the heart of these organizations. When members are inducted, they agree to abide by the rules and regulations of the family, including maintaining all the secrets they learn over their time within the ranks. If one should choose to leave the family, they will typically be cut off from all benefits they once enjoyed as a member. In other cases, the only way out may be death. So, what is a Mafia and how is it run? Before diving headfirst into the history of the Los Angeles crime family, we will explore exactly what a Mafia is.

Anatomy of a Mafia

To have a thorough understanding of the Los Angeles Mafia crime family, it is crucial to have a solid knowledge base of what a Mafia is and how it's run. At its heart, it is a highly organized unit, much like a chosen family.

The basic definition of a Mafia is a secret criminal organization. It can be related to specific traffic, such as cocaine, or a place like Sicily (*Definition of Mafia*, n.d.). Initially, the term "mafioso" referred to a member of the Mafia in Sicily but had no criminal allusions.

Instead, it was used to indicate individuals who were suspicious of any form of central authority.

Within a Mafia, there are general terms used in conversations by members of the organization. These common terms include the following:

- La Cosa Nostra
- omertà
- capo
- family
- wiseguy

La Cosa Nostra has different meanings, depending on the source of the translation. It is often used to indicate "our thing" or "our way." The United States government also uses the term to refer to the American Mafia (Alexander, 2022).

One of the primary beliefs of any Mafia is the strict code of silence or omertà. No matter what happens, any member is expected to keep quiet about any criminal activity. This means they will face all consequences of being caught, including going to jail or worse, without ever revealing any of the Mafia's secrets. In most cases, those who break this rule are subject to forfeiting their own lives if the Mafia members were to get their hands on them. However, exceptions have been made, including in the case of Carmen Milano, who we will cover in greater detail in later chapters.

The family is the structure of the Mafia. It is made of the individual parts of the organization, including the capos, who are the equivalent of military captains who command their soldiers and the non-made members of the family, the associates. The capos are ranking members of the family. Wiseguy was another commonly used term to refer to a made man or a member of the Mafia ranks.

There are several important roles within a Mafia—more than just the capos. From the top to the bottom, key roles make up the family. The organization is highly structured, with different ranks reporting to those above them, much like in a formal business setting.

At the top is the boss, who is responsible for making all the decisions for the family. This position's authority is used to keep order among the ranks and resolve any disputes that arise. The majority of the Mafia's income will also come to the boss. While this is the ultimate position of power, the man who holds it must be wise and know how to play politics. After all, going up against the wrong enemy could prove fatal, even for the boss.

The role beneath the boss is the underboss. This is the boss's right-hand man, and it's his right to choose this person. The underboss is also in a position to arbitrate disputes but will occasionally consult the boss when needed to resolve the most challenging ones. An underboss's power will vary based on the family. Some are groomed and prepared to become the family's next boss, especially if the current one is in a situation where he may no longer be able to rule with his iron fist. He will generally take over the family if the boss becomes incapacitated due to being incarcerated or because of a health issue.

Placed between the boss and underboss is the consigliere. This individual is meant to be an advisor to the boss and is considered someone without the ambition to advance or gain power within the family. Because of this, the consigliere is believed to be on the side of what is right instead of his own or the boss's interests. This position was designed as a form of protection for the average member of the family and, as such, is an elected position and not an appointed one.

The capos are chosen by the boss, and the number in place depends on the total size of the family. Each capo runs their own operation of soldiers and associates. This crew can vary widely in size from capo to capo. The capo's power will vary based on several factors. Those who are related to the boss will typically enjoy a much greater influence. Additionally, the more powerful money-makers will receive more respect from the family. However, when too many mistakes are made or loyalties are questioned, a capo can be removed from power through demotion or execution.

Soldiers are the lowest level of official family members. They are formally recognized members of the Mafia ranks but are at the bottom of the barrel when it comes to the hierarchy. The soldier's job is to make money and give part of it to his capo. He will do whatever it takes to make that money, including committing murder.

Beneath the soldiers are the associates. These are the absolute lowest level of the Mafia and are not considered made men. They do the grunt work at the order of the made members of the family. As their name implies, associates work alongside made men in various criminal enterprises. While they are not official members of the family, if they meet all the criteria, they have the potential to become made men.

In order to enter a Mafia, one must meet several criteria. First and foremost, only men are allowed to join the ranks, even as associates.

In fact, women are meant to be kept completely out of the circle of criminal activities. Regardless of who they may be in a relationship with or what rank their partner is, women are not allowed to have inner knowledge of the Mafia. That said, when it comes to dating, there are also stringent rules around being involved with the female family members of made men. Women who are not related to Mafia members have no restrictions placed on them other than being kept out of the loop regarding all knowledge of the family's activities.

Second, to be eligible, the man must have an Italian father. In some cases, the families are even stricter, requiring that both parents have an Italian heritage. If an individual's father is already a member of the Mafia, he will likely have an easier time gaining entry to the ranks.

Additionally, he must also prove his worth in the money-making game. If he cannot produce enough income to make himself a valuable asset, he will not become a made man. Many are ready, willing, and able to commit murders for the family; however, they're generally incapable of producing regular income that can be passed onto the capos.

Most who want to join the official ranks of the family will also be expected to participate in a murder. They won't necessarily have to be the one who pulls the trigger, but they must be willing to take on that role. However, there have been exceptions over the years where not every associate has been required to be part of a murder to become a member.

Once an associate is deemed worthy of acceptance into the fold, they will be inducted into the family in a formal ceremony. This information was once highly coveted and only known to the made men of the ranks until specific individuals were called to testify before the United States government.

At the time when an associate will be inducted into the Mafia, his capo will notify him that he needs to get "dressed up," which is the signal that the ceremony will take place. In most cases, the prospective member will be brought before a gathering of the ranks of official members of the family. The family members are allowed the opportunity to clear the air of any problems they have with the person before he is formally inducted. However, it should be noted that this is a pure formality—anything serious would have prevented them from ever getting to the point of this meeting.

Generally, during the ceremony, the new member is paired with a senior member who will be his mentor as he assimilates into his new position in the ranks. He will also take an oath in which he declares his desire to join the Mafia to protect his loved ones. He also swears that he will never condemn the family or disobey an order, no matter the circumstances. Many ceremonies have been described in legal testimony and have included the description of the boss burning a piece of paper during the process as a representation of the inductee's soul burning should he betray the family to the authorities at any time (Capeci, 2002). In some situations, the ceremonies will be cut short. This can happen when the family is in a time of war with another family or similar circumstances.

After his induction, the new member is introduced to the rules of the family. It is expected that these rules will be obeyed with a failure to comply being punishable by death. The intended purpose of these rules is to protect the family and maintain its secrets.

The primary rule everyone must follow is that of omertà. Keeping the silence is a requirement from the top to the bottom. No matter what happens, it is expected that the individual in question will not turn to the authorities and will not divulge any family secrets should he be caught, even if it means a lesser sentence. However, it is clear that this rule has been broken several times over the decades, with most of the knowledge of the inner workings of the Mafia coming from members who opted to turn state's evidence in exchange for lesser sentences.

A story behind omertà says it was formed by the Italian Mafias to protect their ranks and families from corrupt authorities. Furthermore, this secrecy was backed by critically severe punishments to ensure no members betrayed the outfit. Eventually, the American Mafias incorporated omertà for a slightly different reason—they were protecting themselves from legitimate government rules, actions, and regulations (Capeci, 2002).

Once someone joins a Mafia, they are expected to understand that nothing, including their own family, comes before it. Because of this, when they are given a direct order from a superior, they're expected to follow through without a hitch, complaint, or hesitation. In fact, noncompliance could result in the member's death.

It is expected that when an associate is summoned, they will respond promptly. This is one of the first lessons learned following their induction and acceptance to the position of soldier. Unfortunately for the individual, it is also a convenient method to summon someone about to be murdered by the family for any perceived infraction of the rules.

Additionally, when a direction is given to carry out a murder, it doesn't matter who the target is, even if it is the person's family member or close friend. If they fail to complete the task, their life will be considered forfeit. As you will soon see, throughout the history of the Los Angeles crime family, several situations arose in which members were ordered to take out their close friends. In some cases, the orders would be followed, while in others, the member would stall indefinitely.

Another crucial rule all members must adhere to is maintaining the utmost respect for all member's female relations. This includes their girlfriends. Single, unrelated women are not encompassed by this rule.

Members are also supposed to have respect for one another with physical boundaries. With this rule, they are expected to not slap, push, shove, or punch one another. The intention is to keep the violence among members to a minimum. Senior ranking members intervene to alleviate the tension and resolve the conflict when violations happen. Major disputes have occurred over the result of this rule being broken and one of those involved not agreeing with the senior member's ruling.

No soldier or associate is allowed to embark on any activity without requesting the permission of their capo. This can range from interacting with other members to attempting to make money on their own. Additionally, they cannot just plan a vacation outside their turf without permission. By establishing this rule, the Mafia helps to maintain order and prevents conflicts with other mobsters. Failing to alert a capo to a plan to make money can result in the associate or soldier's death should they be found out. Additionally, it prevents turf wars among the families should the soldier or associate encroach on territory where they should not be.

There was also an attempt to implement a rule that eliminated drug trafficking and dealing. However, many Mafia members continued to participate in this activity. The reason behind the restriction was the government's crackdown on the activity in the 1950s. The Mafia didn't want to lose its secret support with law enforcement and government agents through this illegal trade. However, many continued down this path and proceeded to be caught. Because of this, the actual rule can be considered more of the members needing to avoid being caught selling drugs (Capeci, 2002).

At the end of the day, the primary rule for all members is to make money and pass it up the chain to their superiors. After all, the Mafia is a money-making organization at its heart. If members cannot produce, they're not needed, placing them in a position to be permanently removed.

The Roots of the Sicilian Mafia

Most scholars agree that the Mafia originated on the island of Sicily during the 19th century. However, some disagree, stating that the origins date back to the Middle Ages. In this latter interpretation of the origins, it is believed the Mafia was developed to overthrow the invading forces that were taking over the island. These forces included invaders from Spain and Norway (Britannica, 2019).

Absentee landlords hired private armies known as *mafie* to protect their landed estates. This protection was much sought after due to the roving bandits that plagued Sicily throughout the ages. In the 18th and 19th centuries, the tides turned with the members of these armies turning on the landowners and extorting money from them in exchange for this protection (Britannica, 2019).

The Mafia has been considered a traditional part of Sicilian culture for many years, ranging from the end of the 19th century to the middle of the 20th century. Its societal role was an expression of the individual's need to express anti-authoritarian assertiveness. This was deeply associated with a Sicilian pattern of behavior and way of life (Benigno, 2018).

Despite the various foreign governments that ruled over Sicily throughout the centuries, the Mafia survived because these governments ruled with such oppression that the Mafia's way of order appeared significantly more tolerable. By 1900, the Mafia families who were based in western Sicily's villages had developed a confederation of sorts that allowed them to monopolize the economic activities of their geographic locations (Britannica, 2019).

The Sicilian Mafia was not the only one to develop in Italy, as there were also the Camorra and Calabrian Mafias. However, the Sicilian Mafia is considered the grandfather of all Mafias.

Eventually, the Sicilian Mafia would spread to the United States. The first known member of the Mafia to emigrate was Giuseppe Esposito. He and six other Sicilians fled the island seeking refuge in New York following the murder of a vice chancellor and 11 landowners. In 1881, he was arrested in New Orleans and extradited back to Italy to stand up for his crimes (Alexander, 2022).

The Rise of the Mafias in Italy

Italy became a unified country, and Sicily joined it in 1861. Despite this merger, crime continued to be a widespread problem across the island as the new government established its footing. Because the crime resulted in such a high degree of chaos, Roman officials sought out the Mafia in the 1870s for help. They struck a bargain in which the Sicilian Mafia families would target independent criminal groups in exchange for the government turning a blind eye to the shakedowns of landowners.

While the government officials established this agreement, believing it would be temporary, the results were astonishingly opposite of their expectations. Rome wanted to regain control of the country through the use of Mafia power. Instead, the government enabled the Mafia to expand its criminal activities, deepening the clans' hold on the Sicilian economy and politics.

As the Mafia gained power in politics, the members became professionals at political corruption. They pressured people to vote for their chosen candidates who were under their control. The Catholic Church was also heavily intertwined with the Mafia throughout this time. Church officials relied on the Mafia clans to protect their property holdings in Sicily, keeping the tenant farmers in line at all times (History.com Editors, 2019).

In order to further strengthen themselves, Sicilian clans began conducting initiation ceremonies in which new members pledged secret oaths of loyalty. Of chief importance to the clans was omerta, an all-important code of conduct reflecting the ancient Sicilian belief that a person should never go to government authorities to seek justice for a crime and never cooperate with authorities investigating any wrongdoing. (History.com Editors, 2019)

Expanding to the United States

Toward the end of the 19th century and the beginning of the 20th century, many unskilled laborers, craftsmen, and farmers from Italy made their way to America in search of better opportunities. The number of Italians in New York alone skyrocketed between 1880 and 1910. Eventually, this group comprised one-tenth of the city's population (History.com Editors, 2018).

While many of these immigrants lived their lives within the confines of American laws, others brought the ways of the Sicilian Mafia with them, forming gangs that often preyed upon their own neighborhoods. This behavior continued into the 1920s when the Prohibition era occurred, with many of these gangs becoming proficient at the illegal trade and smuggling of alcohol. They expanded their illegal activities to include money laundering and bribing law enforcement and public officials (History.com Editors, 2018).

"In the late 1920s, a bloody power struggle known as the Castellammarese War broke out between New York City's two biggest Italian-American criminal gangs. In 1931, after the faction led by Sicilian-born crime boss Salvatore Maranzano (1886-1931) came out on top, he crowned himself the 'capo di tutti capi,' or boss of all bosses, in New York" (History.com Editors, 2018b). Lucky Luciano was rising in power around that time and didn't appreciate the power grab that Maranzano made. In retaliation, Luciano had him killed in 1931. He then went on to be the mastermind behind the formation of The Commission, which was essentially the national American Mafia board of directors. At that time, there were 20 active families nationwide.

At this same time in Italy, the Sicilian Mafia was under attack from Benito Mussolini. He viewed the Mafia members as a direct threat to his rule, and many were imprisoned. However, many also escaped, looking for freedom in the United States. These men became part of the bootlegging industry and the ever-growing American Mafia. The two criminal organizations were entirely separate; however, the American Mafia took on many aspects of its Sicilian counterpart, including omertà.

Throughout the first half of the 20th century, the Mafia spread throughout the United States. Five crime families established themselves in New York City alone. These families included the following:

- Bonanno
- Colombo
- Gambino
- Genovese
- Lucchese

With their proximity to one another, tensions have been high, as each family has tried to control the city. They have all been established for more than 100 years. In all other cities where there was Mafia activity, only one family would establish itself. Each of the five families were given a vote on The Commission after it was established.

While there were plenty of opportunities for the Mafia families to spread and stake their claims in the United States, the time of Prohibition would be their biggest money maker. Additionally, it would be the start of the Los Angeles Mafia crime family.

CHAPTER 1

PROHIBITION AND THE FOUNDING OF THE LOS ANGELES CRIME FAMILY

Decades before the start of Prohibition, criminal gangs lived in society. However, Prohibition was the gateway for the mobs to take control of organized crime in America. In fact, *organized crime* was a term that technically didn't even develop until this era began.

Before the 18th Amendment was passed in 1919 with the ban of intoxicating liquor sales following, shortly after in January 1920, corrupt political bosses led the organized crime world, not the Mafia. Gangs were under the thumb of political candidates, pressuring opponents and swaying the vote toward the bosses. In return, their illegal activities were ignored by law enforcement and politicians (History.com Editors, 2018).

As Prohibition was established, the power shifted tremendously. Despite being illegal, the desire for a drink didn't diminish. Someone had to supply it, and who better than the Mafia?

Bootlegging and the Prohibition

The 18th Amendment banned all sales and imports of alcohol in all forms beginning in 1920, starting the Prohibition era. This continued for more than a decade until the government repealed the Amendment in 1933. Because it removed the legal sale of alcohol, the demand for illicit supply immediately arose.

Anti-alcohol sentiment in the United States at the time dated back to the 1800s. Many sought the ban of the substance due to the belief that it caused problems such as inefficiency, laziness, and the end of family life. The temperance movement, primarily led by Christian women's groups, heavily lobbied for Prohibition while standing firmly against saloons. Women were the primary supporters of Prohibition due to problems with their husbands spending their money on liquor and leaving none for the needs of the children. "In the 1870s, inspired by the rising indignation of Methodist and Baptist clergymen, and by distraught wives and mothers whose lives had been ruined by the excesses of the saloon, thousands of women began to protest and organize politically for the cause of temperance. Their organization, the Women's Christian Temperance Union (WCTU), became a force to be reckoned with, their cause enhanced by alliance with Susan B. Anthony, Elizabeth Cady Stanton, and other women battling for the vote" (*Prohibition and Organized Crime*, 2015).

In 1846, Maine passed prohibition legislation and was followed by several other states. Eventually, the temperance movement proved successful with the passing of the 18th Amendment and the institution of Prohibition. This law, also known as the Volstead Act, made the transportation, sale, and production of alcohol illegal nationwide. An interesting fact about the law is that it didn't ban the consumption or possession of alcohol, but it essentially made it impossible to legally purchase it (Sullivan, 2014). With legal sources of obtaining liquor eradicated, those who wanted a drink were quick to find other sources, even if they were risky.

Wayne Wheeler would lead the formation of the Anti-Saloon League (ASL) in 1893. The ASL would become the most successful lobbying organization in the country. The members were willing to join forces with any constituencies that shared the same goals. They united with everyone, from the Democrats and Republicans to the National Association for the Advancement of Colored People (NAACP) and the Ku Klux Klan (KKK). In general, the staunchest supporters were the farmers.

While their intentions were to complete a societal transformation for the better, temperance activists didn't achieve the results they were hoping for. From the very early stages of Prohibition, many found ways to produce and sell alcohol in secret. Others produced their own homebrews, including moonshine. Unfortunately, these brews were not always the safest for consumption, making them extremely risky to drink. Despite the risks and potential hazards, illegal alcohol production and sales opportunities paved the way for the country's rise in organized crime (Sullivan, 2014).

Additionally, the 18th Amendment made the average person a common criminal for seeking to buy alcohol. There were never enough police to begin with to enforce the new law, ensuring the mobsters had nearly free reign with their illegal sales and importation operations.

Bootlegging was the "illegal traffic in liquor in violation of legislative restrictions on its manufacture, sale, or transportation" (*Bootlegging | Definition, History, & Facts*, 2017). The word originated in the 1880s in the Midwest in relation to concealing flasks of illegal liquor to trade with the Native Americans. It gained more widespread use during the Prohibition era, where it became a lucrative racket, or illegal money-making activity, for the gangs that would become the American Mafia. Before the 18th Amendment was passed and the Mafia came into power, the most organized criminal schemes in the country were managed by corrupt political bosses. Bootlegging would spur the changes necessary for the Mafia crime families to take over organized crime.

The earliest practice of bootlegging during Prohibition involved bringing supplies over the borders from Canada and Mexico. The bootleggers also used ships along the seacoast with their favorite suppliers being from Cuba, the Bahamas, Sainte-Pierre, and Miquelon. The rum runners had a favorite spot to rendezvous just offshore from Atlantic City, New Jersey, which was outside the government's jurisdiction. They would load their freight into a craft that was faster than the U.S. Coast Guard boats, allowing them to quickly get away (*Bootlegging | Definition, History, & Facts*, 2017).

Eventually, the Coast Guard upped its game, beginning to execute searches farther out and using higher-speed boats. As this method of smuggling became more and more dangerous, bootleggers began using other methods. These included obtaining supplies of medicinal whiskey that were sold with valid and fraudulent prescriptions, denatured alcohol used by various industries, and homemade alcohol manufactured from corn. Much of the denatured alcohol had to be cleaned of poisonous chemicals that were added to prevent people from drinking it. Once that was completed, it was sold to speakeasies or individuals. Liquor made from corn often posed a severe health risk when it was incorrectly distilled, leading to blindness, paralysis, or death (*Bootlegging | Definition, History, & Facts*, 2017).

Because bootlegging required significantly more organization than many other crimes, organized gangs developed that would control entire operations, including the distilleries, storage, transport, and outlets. They focused on securing their territories and expanding to create monopolies. With the rise of bootlegging, gang violence dramatically increased. There were a significant number of wars and murders between rival gangs, with one of the most notable being the Saint Valentine's Day Massacre of 1929 in Chicago. In this incident, the Al Capone gang shot and killed seven members of the George "Bugs" Moran gang.

"The demand for illegal beer, wine, and liquor was so great during the Prohibition that mob kingpins like Capone were pulling in as much as $100 million a year in the mid-1920s ($1.4 billion in 2018) and spending a half million dollars a month in bribes to police, politicians and federal investigators" (Roos, 2019). The mobsters had to think outside the box to become businessmen. The money flow was so great that they needed a way to keep up and keep it secret. With their gun-handling abilities and intimidation tactics, they were well-equipped to protect their speakeasies, breweries, and rum-running operations from rivals. They also had the means for security in their establishments and knew how to effectively bribe anyone who would shut them down. The money was a different story—they needed lawyers and accountants to launder it for them. Ultimately, they also needed to forge partnerships with rival gangs to solidify their investments. These partnerships resulted in peace across multiple areas as they learned to work with one another instead of focusing on the bloodbath they once lived for.

As their cooperation with one another increased, they expanded their criminal activities from bootlegging to include prostitution rings, loan sharking, narcotics trafficking, gambling, extortion, and labor racketeering. Finally, in the late 1920s and early 1930s, the American Mafia arose from the activities of the Italian bootleggers in New York City.

During the Prohibition era, some of the most lucrative bootlegging operations involved importing illegal alcohol from Canada via the Great Lakes. Arnold Rothstein, famous underworld profiteer who fixed the 1919 World Series, ran his shipments through Lake Ontario, down the Hudson River, and onward to the New York City speakeasies. In Cleveland, the Mayfield Road Gang famously ran their rum-running speedboats across Lake Erie.

Despite the 18th Amendment being repealed in 1933, many counties and jurisdictions maintained a state of prohibition. Because of this, bootlegging activities didn't end. Those who found this criminal activity to be lucrative continued to thrive.

It's clear that Prohibition had a significant transformative effect on the mob. In fact, before Prohibition, the members of the Sicilian Mafia in places like New York City, Kansas City, New Orleans, and Chicago made their money through a racket called the Black Hand. They would demand payments from other Italians with cryptic letters that involved threats of violence and death. These notes had mysterious black hands, daggers, or other symbols printed on them. One of the most notorious users of the Black Hand methods was Ignazio Saietta, known as Lupo or the Wolf in the Little Italy district of Manhattan. However, he was apprehended in 1920 for counterfeiting and sentenced to 30 years in prison. Lieutenant Joseph Petrosino was the most notable enemy of the Black Hand rackets. He worked for the New York Police Department and had many gang members arrested, jailed, or deported before his own murder in 1909 when he went on a trip to Palermo, Sicily. The activity of the Black Hand dramatically declined with the advent of Prohibition. As crime became more organized, there was no need for cryptic threats to obtain money when a fortune could be made through illegal trade.

With the end of Prohibition, the gangs changed tactics from bootlegging to their secondary operations, including prostitution, drugs, and gambling. When the Great Depression rolled around, they were the ones with the money while everyone else was left without. If someone wanted to start a business, the only recourse was to turn to organized crime and seek out a loan shark. So, while the Prohibition movement aimed to reform a powerfully negative tendency in the country, it ended up birthing what would become one of the worst criminal traditions the nation would ever have.

The Founding of the Los Angeles Crime Family

In the early 20th century, organized crime in California was mainly made up of various Italian street gangs who employed the Black Hand extortion methods. The Matranga family was a leader among these gangs. They "were a family of Arbereshe origin from an Albanian noble family which settled in south Italy hundreds of years ago" (*Los Angeles Crime Family*, 2023). It was run by the family of Charles Matranga, who was the founder of the New Orleans crime family. While they had a legitimate fruit vending business, their main criminal activities boiled down to arson, threats, extortion, and violence. Through these methods, they exerted control over the Plaza area, which was the central focus of the Italian community in Los Angeles during that period. Rosario "Sam" Matranga was the first leader of the family, establishing control in 1905. His name has often been mistaken for Orsario due to an error on his death records. He was joined by his relatives Pietro "Peter" Matranga, Salvatore Matranga, and Antonio "Tony" Matranga (*Los Angeles Crime Family - Origins and Predecessors*, n.d.).

Joseph Ardizzone was one of the first known bosses of the Los Angeles Mafia crime family. He's also credited with the first organized crime murder in Los Angeles. In 1906, as a prominent Black Hand leader, he was involved in a feud with George Maisano, who he would shoot in the back and kill outside the Maler Brewery. Maisano was a friend of the Matranga family, which meant Ardizzone was in for retribution for his crime. Because of this, he temporarily fled the state, avoiding authorities and the Matranga family. Ardizzone used an alias, picked up odd jobs here and there, and traveled the country. Eventually, he settled on farming in Louisville for some time. While he was gone, those out to get him had no means of reaching him and instead focused on his friends and family.

Within the enclaves of Los Angeles was a well-known and trusted arbiter of disputes, Joseph "Uncle Joe" Cuccia. His advice was sought after whenever there were disputes between landowners and fruit vendors. However, he was much more than that, as he was a translator for the Italians in courtroom settings. Because of this, he was well liked and respected within the Italian community. Uncle Joe would have been the one to make the final decision about the outcome of the dispute between Ardizzone and Maisano. Because the ruling was not in Maisano's favor, he spread rumors of favoritism due to a blood relation between Uncle Joe and Ardizzone because Ardizzone's mother was originally a Cuccia. Courtroom testimony would later reveal that Maisano openly threatened Ardizzone's life, leading Ardizzone to act first to prevent his own death. Despite this, the disrespect shown toward Uncle Joe likely profoundly impacted Ardizzone's decision to act brazenly (Niotta, 2018).

The role of the arbiter was much like that of the consigliere and is considered to be a position deserving of much respect among the Italians and Sicilians across the country. One such example was Gaspar "The Peacekeeper" Milazzo from Detroit. Several men in this position would travel the country to squash these internal squabbles amongst family members or between different groups. Some also served as the bearers of messages that were best delivered face to face. The position was granted significant authority, with at least one arbiter filling in as an acting boss for a family. Uncle Joe filled the role until his death when Jack Dragna stepped in. The difference with Dragna was that he came with an official title into the unofficial role. "As a founder and leading member of the city's prohibition era protective association, the Italian Welfare League, Dragna became known as the Mayor of the Italian Ghettos" (Niotta, 2018).

In the early 1930s, Milazzo and Dragna were a part of the Castellammarese War, which was an internal struggle within the membership ranks of La Cosa Nostra. Eventually, this would pave the way for the American Mafia. In 1930, Gaspar Milazzo and his driver attended a sitdown intended to diffuse a situation of bad blood to ease the tension among the enclaves of Castellammare del Golfo, Sicily. Instead of achieving their goal, they were gunned down. In a similar situation, Uncle Joe Cuccia became the target of the Matranga family due to his involvement in the arbitration of the disagreement between Maisano and Ardizzone. Maisano clung to life for about two months following the shooting before finally dying. After that, Uncle Joe became what was likely the first drive-by shooting in Los Angeles history. Before the end of the following year, on New Year's Eve 1907, Giovannino Bentivegna was gunned down in his barber shop as another Matranga attack on Ardizzone's associates.

Joe Ardizzone made his return to California in 1912, but authorities had no idea he was there until they received a complaint from one of his neighbors. He had allegedly been courting their underage teenage daughter, who he would later end up marrying. In 1914, they surrounded the ranch he established in Southland, taking him in for his crimes. He remained incarcerated for a year throughout the trial for George Maisano's murder but was ultimately released on a self-defense verdict in 1915.

Following the trial, hatred was still high between the Matrangas and Ardizzones, resulting in a war that would amass a sizable body count. In most of the murders, the weapon of choice was the shotgun, which resulted in many nearly decapitated bodies. In other cases, the victims' remains were simply never found. Joe Ardizzone gained allies by either forming or joining the North End Gang. The members included Ardizzone's brothers and their cousins from the Borgia and Cuccia sides of the family. The gang's gunman, Mike Marino (also known as Mike Rizzo), was credited with the murders of Sam and Peter Matranga in 1917. Tony Buccola became the next leader of the Matranga family and was able to get revenge by killing Marino in 1919. However, the damage had been done, and the family was critically weakened by all the violence. Ironically, Ardizzone was the last man standing among the original organized crime members who began the war.

Another significant influence during this period was Vito Di Giorgio, a well-known Black Handler. He originally immigrated to the United States in 1904 from Palermo, Sicily. Later in 1920, he relocated from New Orleans to Los Angeles. While the Ardizzones and Matrangas were still enmeshed in their feud, Di Giorgio helped bring order back to the city's organized crime. "Di Giorgio was known as an intimidating and forceful man who was in conflict with several local underworld factions. Di Giorgio maintained strong connections with mobsters in New Orleans, Colorado, and Chicago, and was a cousin, close friend, and mob associate of New York City mobster Giuseppe Morello, the first boss of the Morello crime family" (*Los Angeles Crime Family*, 2023). He was ultimately killed in 1922 while getting a haircut after surviving two other attempts on his life.

Rosario DeSimone had relocated to Los Angeles from Pueblo, Colorado when Di Giorgio did and was established as his right-hand man. He was a significant power figure although he mainly remained out of the city. He ran his bootlegging operations quietly within Los Angeles County. With Di Giorgio's death, he became the leader of what would become the Los Angeles crime family. He would not hold the position long.

As Prohibition was established nationwide, Ardizzone and his associates capitalized on the opportunity. The reins of the organization were handed over to him from Rosario DeSimone, making him the boss of the Los Angeles crime family. His right-hand man was Jack Dragna, born Ignazio Dragna in 1891 in Sicily. Dragna headed the bootlegging operations throughout the southern parts of the state. Their organization engaged in bootlegging wars with Eastern organized crime outfits that attempted to gain control over their territory.

During the 1920s and 1930s, the development of organized crime in California was very similar to that of the East Coast. Organized crime syndicates emerged in both areas due to Prohibition to supply the masses with illicit alcohol. Their success depended on control of the manufacture and distribution of alcohol. In addition to Dragna, Anthony Cornero was another big name in the bootlegging industry in California. Cornero was no stranger to being arrested and had attained the moniker of "Bootleg King." Several Eastern crime family members moved to the West Coast to attempt to extort those involved in the illegal enterprise. Many believed these gangsters belonged to Al Capone's Chicago family.

In addition to their successful bootlegging operations, Ardizzone and Dragna branched into the realm of gambling and extortion. Toward the end of the 1920s, Ardizzone's power, influence, and control were rapidly expanding. With his leadership, organized crime made significant strides toward consolidation. He was a dominating force in the world of Los Angeles criminal activities. In the late 1920s, Dragna, working with Johnny Roselli, was in constant battle with Charlie Crawford over several lucrative bootlegging operations. With the deaths of his rivals, Buccola and DiCiolla, he became the undisputed leader of organized crime within the city. He was also the prime suspect in their murders.

Around this time, Ardizzone also established the Italian Protective League, which was sometimes called the Italian Welfare League. Jack Dragna was established as the president while Ardizzone took on the role of vice president. They also named State Senator Joseph Pedrotti as the organization's chairman. There were some political and social motives behind the League; however, its main purpose was to function as strong-arm muscle for the Los Angeles crime family.

Joseph Ardizzone Mysteriously Vanishes

Multiple attempts were made on Joe Ardizzone's life following the threats made by George Maisano and the Matrangas. In 1931, Ardizzone was shot at by gunmen when he was with Jimmy Basile. The pair were on their way home from a dinner at Rosario DeSimone's home when the gunmen overtook them in a sedan, firing shotguns. While Ardizzone was the primary target, he was only wounded, but Basile was killed. Ardizzone reportedly made his way back to DeSimone's home with seven gunshot wounds to his back. DeSimone's son was a physician, and he performed first aid until an ambulance arrived to transport Ardizzone to Hollywood Hospital. Authorities believed that the hit was in retaliation for the recent murder of Dominic DiCiolla, the so-called "king" of the Little Italy underworld in the north end of Los Angeles (Hunt, 2019).

Then, in the hospital, another attempt on his life was made. At this time, he decided to leave the Mafia permanently. However, his decision was clearly made too late, as he disappeared on October 15, 1931. That day, Ardizzone was on his way to pick up his cousin Nick Borgia who had arrived from Italy and was staying at a ranch in Etiwanda. His brother filed a missing person's report the following day, and the local authorities began their search. It extended down a 50-mile stretch and was conducted over the course of a week. When they found no hint of his whereabouts, they deemed his disappearance the result of a Mafia hit. His body was never found, and he was "presumed to be the victim of a gangland-style execution" (Younger, 1978). At the time, he was in direct conflict with the Mafia's National Crime Syndicate, likely leading to his demise.

With Ardizzone gone, there was room for a new boss to take over the Los Angeles crime family. His right-hand man, Jack Dragna, stepped up to the plate.

CHAPTER 2

THE JACK DRAGNA ERA

With the disappearance of Joe Ardizzone, Jack Dragna was the next man in succession for the role of boss. Because of Ardizzone's disagreement with the Commission, it was always suspected that it was a sanctioned hit, with Dragna having something to do with it if not being entirely behind it. With Ardizzone out of the picture, the other Mafia leaders readily welcomed Dragna into the fold as the new boss of the Los Angeles crime family. He has been recognized as the most successful boss of the family throughout its entire history, from making peace with the National Mafia Syndicate to receiving a coveted spot on the Commission. But who was Jack Dragna and what made him so successful?

The Los Angeles Crime Family's New Boss

Jack Dragna was born in Corleone, Sicily on April 18, 1891. His parents were Francesco Paolo and Anna Dragna, and his official birth name was Ignazio Dragna. He emigrated to the United States on November 18, 1898, with his family, including his sister Giuseppa and brother Gaetano. The family stayed in East Harlem with the family of Antonio Rizzotto, one of Anna's cousins who was also from Corleone. Dragna remained with his family in New York

City for ten years. At that time, he returned to Sicily, where he joined the Italian Army and later the Sicilian Mafia.

Dragna made his return to the United States in 1914 and applied for naturalization under the name Charles Dragna. He was believed to have a business relationship with Gaetano Reina, who would ultimately lead his criminal organization within New York City in Manhattan and the Bronx. Dragna was the suspect in the murder of Barnet Baff, a Jewish poultry dealer, which led to him fleeing to California. Despite being extradited to New York, he never faced a trial for the crime. In 1915, he would face charges and prison time for another crime—the Black Hand extortion of a man residing in Long Beach. When he was arrested, the name he was filed under was Ignazio Rizzotto. This led to the belief that he was Benigno Rizzotto's brother.

As the Prohibition Era began, Dragna and his brother Gaetano, then known by the name Tom, began working together to produce and sell illegal alcohol in very successful bootlegging operations. He wed his second cousin, Francesca Rizzotto, in 1922 before starting his close relationship with Joseph Ardizzone. In the early stages of Prohibition, he partnered with other key figures to squash the ongoing problems between the various Sicilian clans throughout Los Angeles. These clans ultimately fell under one unified organized family known as the Los Angeles Brugad. The leaders in order of succession of this organization were Vito Di Giorgio, Rosario DeSimone, Joseph Ardizzone, and Jack Dragna. However, Dragna would be recognized as the most powerful and influential force to head the organization for the quarter-century he was in charge of. It is broadly accepted that Ardizzone severely upset the Syndicate, causing his own demise and leading to the Dragna era of the family. Once Dragna was in charge, he established his brother Tom as his consigliere, and later, his nephew Louis Tom Dragna was initiated as a made man in 1947.

Several sources discount the Los Angeles Mafia as having enough influence to be part of the formation of the New York Commission or send members to attend its meetings. However, Nicola Gentile, a high-ranking La Cosa Nostra member, and federal documentation refute these claims. According to Gentile, "the first to go to the restaurant, which had been chosen by [Salvatore] Maranzano, were the representatives of California and the far West, ten in all" (Niotta, n.d.). This meant that they put in the effort to travel the distance and were the first to make an appearance at the meeting point. Several informants revealed that Dragna was in attendance at many meetings of the higher-ranking Mafia members on the East Coast during the 1930s.

It's commonly accepted that Dragna never established his own foothold in Las Vegas; however, he can be credited with having a significant impact on the formation of Sin City. Dragna and his organization ousted the founding fathers of the Las Vegas we know today from Los Angeles. He worked closely with long-time associate John Roselli to drive this older gambling syndicate out of the city. Dragna and Roselli also partnered with Joe Shaw, Mayor Frank Shaw's brother, to push out the Los Angeles bookmakers, who would mostly end up relocating to Las Vegas. The founding fathers of Las Vegas made up the Spring Street Combination and were well-established as gamblers and racketeers in the city before they relocated to the southern reaches of Nevada. Members of the

Combination included Guy McAfee, Luther "Tutor" Scherer, Kent Kane Parrot, Milton "Farmer" Page, Zeke Caress, Albert "Black" Marco, Chuck Addison, "Good Time" Charlie Crawford, and Eddie Nealis. They ran their operations with the assistance of a puppet mayor, George Cryer (Niotta, n.d.).

The Italian clans were a significant thorn in the side of the Combination for many years, impacting their bootlegging operations. Things became even worse for the organization when Ardizzone and Dragna entered the political realm in the mid-1920s. During this time, the pair formed the Italian Welfare League. When Dragna assumed control of the Los Angeles Brugad in 1931, the Combination faced even more problems. Dragna and his brother used all-out war tactics to carve out a solid piece of the city specifically for the Italians. They forced their way into the gambling rackets, taking charge of operations. Eventually, the Combination was forced to pay out to the Italians to continue their prostitution and gambling activities within Los Angeles for the remainder of the 1930s. The Combination finally made its exit from the city in 1938 and 1938, moving on to create the elaborate world of Las Vegas. While other factors were at play, this move may never have happened if Dragna and his associates had not played a significant role in the political realm.

Chief Sources of Income

During Dragna's reign, the Los Angeles crime family had several sources of income. While Dragna is recognized as the most influential leader of the organization, he was never able to get an established foothold in many of the entertainment industry's labor unions. However, this didn't prevent him from involving the family in the entertainment business. Dragna also had the honor of being the only Mafia boss west of Chicago to receive a position on The Commission, the governing body of the American Mafia system. By the end of Prohibition in 1933, his business interests had expanded to include loansharking and illegal gambling. Additionally, with the removal of the Spring Street Combination to Nevada, the Los Angeles crime family became the controlling hand in the world of illicit gambling throughout the city.

While illegal gambling was a lucrative source of income for the family, Dragna's primary funding came from extorting protection money from the local independent bookmakers. These were the individuals who sports bettors went through to attempt to gain their riches in high-stakes games or races. The family would require these bookies to make a payout to receive their protection from others—not to mention they would be protected from the family itself. At that time, many organized crime members would threaten businesses or bookies who failed to pay their tributes to the organization. These threats would include the promise of violence and were considered a protection racket. Dragna had a much more creative plan to get the independent bookmakers to pay out. The individuals would still have threats against their business from various sources, making them need the protection of the family. However, what they didn't know was that Dragna sent those threats knocking at the door of their businesses to shake them up and convince them they needed to be protected. Through this creative coercion, he had much greater success getting his protection tributes from the bookies.

Dragna and the Los Angela crime family also turned to other means of making money. One method was to run gambling ships. These were operated outside the jurisdiction of local anti-gambling laws. Some were permanently moored offshore, while others would move to and from their gaming locations. Additionally, the family operated a heroin trafficking operation and extorted money from other local businesses. All in all, they had a lucrative money-making setup that afforded Dragna the opportunity to stay out of the limelight. Many believed he was a weak leader because of his desire to remain out of the spotlight. On the other hand, Mickey Cohen said Dragna was well-respected and influential; however, he didn't set up the organization the way the East Coast leaders expected or wanted (*Los Angeles Crime Family*, 2023). Dragna was able to enforce control over a large area throughout California and into Nevada with the aid of several important members. He also established a strong connection with the corrupt force of the Los Angeles County Sheriff's Department and infiltrated some of the unions in the laundromat and dress importation industries.

Uneasy Relations

Unlike the families on the East Coast, they lacked a large pool of Italian men in the community to select for membership in the Los Angeles crime family, so Dragna and his crew had to be creative about boosting their numbers. The family accepted names like "Johnny Roselli from Chicago, Nick Licata from Detroit, and Aladena "Jimmy the Weasel" Fratianno and Dominic Brooklier from Cleveland. Armed with top hitmen Frank Bompensiero and Jimmy Fratianno (who committed over 30 murders on the orders of their superiors), Dragna muscled his way into controlling territory stretching throughout California and Southern Nevada" (*Los Angeles Crime Family*, 2023). His connection with the Los Angeles County Sheriff's Department furthered Dragna's gains throughout the city.

Dragna had close supporters in his business dealings, including Girolamo "Momo" Adamo and John Roselli. Momo had lived in Chicago and Kansas City before relocating to Los Angeles in the 1930s. He would eventually be named as Dragna's underboss. Roselli had been a Chicago Outfit member before he elected to move to Los Angeles, where he became engaged with Dragna in the gambling operations. He would eventually leave California in the 1950s to become the Mafia's primary Las Vegas representative. Dragna also maintained his connection to his old bootlegging partner Cornero, who operated gambling ships off the California coast.

Lucky Luciano of New York and the other Syndicate leaders sent Benjamin "Bugsy" Siegel to the West Coast in 1937 to develop rackets and further their business interests. This included those interests in Las Vegas. Siegel was born on February 28, 1906. He and his childhood friend, Meyer Lansky, were strong influences in the Jewish mob. However, they would also hold significant roles within the Italian-American Mafia as well as the Italian-Jewish National Crime Syndicate. Siegel was one of the founders of Murder, Inc., which was considered to be the strong arm of the National Crime Syndicate. Following his career as a bootlegger during Prohibition, he turned to gambling rackets as his primary source of income. As a mobster, Siegel was well-known for his violent tendencies, which led to him being relied on as a hitman and muscle.

Once he relocated to Los Angeles, an uneasy partnership was formed between Siegel and Dragna. In many records of the period, the two are depicted as enemies, with Dragna in a more subservient role to Siegel. "Some theories even stipulate the powers back East, big names like Lucky Luciano, delivered an ultimatum, personally telling Jack Dragna to stay out of Siegel's way" (Niotta, n.d.).

Regardless of whether those theories were true, Siegel had a knack for getting the independent bookies to pay into Dragna's massively successful gambling operation. The relationship between the two was strained because Dragna envied Siegel's ability to get a foothold in the movie industry's unions. With this infiltration, he was able to extort millions from the production companies, and Dragna only saw a fraction as a tribute for Bugsy working in his territory. In fact, he was able to take over the Screen Extras Guild and the Los Angeles Teamsters. This allowed him to make significant gains off Warner Brothers Studios. Because Siegel was backed by New York and The Commission, Dragna had no say and could not get a handle on their ever-growing grip on the city. It was noted that Siegel's primary purpose for moving to the West Coast was to start a horse racing wire service. The two ended up working together to establish this racket and tried several ways to take over the Continental Press Service, the primary wire service at the time. When all efforts at a takeover failed, they proceeded to open their own wire service, Trans-America. Eventually, the Chicago Outfit would move in and seize control of the rival service, Continental Racing Services. Once this was done, they proceeded to give Dragna the West Coast percentage of the racing wire, which enraged Bugsy (Los Angeles Crime Family, 2023).

While in Hollywood, Siegel also made many famous friends, rubbing elbows with all the right people. "He was known to associate with George Raft, Clark Gable, Gary Cooper and Cary Grant, as well as studio executives Louis B. Mayer and Jack L. Warner. Actress Jean Harlow was a friend of Siegel and godmother to his daughter Millicent" (*Bugsy Siegel*, 2022). He also had relationships with many famous women, including the Countess Dorothy di Frasso. In 1938, di Frasso brought Siegel to Italy, where he was introduced to Benito Mussolini. He attempted to make an arms deal with Mussolini. He also met two Nazi leaders during that trip and offered to kill them until the Countess made several pleas for him to change his mind.

Siegel lived an extravagant lifestyle once he became established in California. "He bought a palatial estate, frequented parties, and rubbed elbows with Hollywood moguls and starlets" (History.com Editors, 2009). He struck up a relationship with actress Virginia Hill. The couple relocated to Las Vegas in 1945 so that Bugsy could begin building his dream of a gambling oasis in the desert. Additionally, the move to Las Vegas was a way for Siegel to rescue his reputation following the trial for the murder of Harry "Big Greenie" Greenberg. On September 22, 1939, Siegel and three accomplices killed Greenberg outside his apartment. Greenberg had threatened to become an informant, making him a risk and resulting in a hit put on him. One of the accomplices, Albert Tannenbaum, confessed to the killing and agreed to testify against Siegel. The case received almost instant notoriety because Siegel received significant preferential treatment while in prison, including visits from females, approved visits to the dentist, and alternative foods. Tannenbaum's testimony was dismissed and two of the state's witnesses died. Without further evidence, no conviction could be made, resulting in Siegel's acquittal in 1942. However, the damage was done. The newspapers all referred to him as "Bugsy," which was a reference to being crazy.

The Syndicate funded his Las Vegas venture, allowing him to break ground on the Flamingo Hotel and Casino. His project was given an initial budget of $1.5 million, but expenses quickly escalated beyond $6 million by 1947. The work was coming to a close by late November 1947, and Siegel's behavior throughout would establish a pattern for future casino moguls. His violent reputation made those around him somewhat uncomfortable. "He boasted one day that he had personally killed some men; he saw the panicked look on the face of head contractor Del Webb and reassured him: 'Del, don't worry, we only kill each other'" (*Bugsy Siegel*, 2022). Despite this interaction, other associates portrayed Siegel as being intense but very charitable. Even his attorney vouched for him, calling him well-liked and saying he was good to others. During this time, the Outfit had cleared up its problems with the wire service in Arizona and Nevada. However, Siegel refused to report on his business operations in California. It was said that he reported to his close associates that he was operating the California syndicate on his own and would return the loans he received at his convenience. Because he had previously proven himself dependable and valuable, the Mafia bosses demonstrated significant patience with Siegel (*Bugsy Siegel*, 2022).

The Flamingo Hotel opened on December 26, 1946, despite not being completed. Few celebrities were in attendance but those who did brave the bad weather were met with a cacophony of construction noise and drop cloths throughout the lobby. Additionally, the hotel boasted the first air conditioning unit of the desert, but it, too, was not up to the job of entertaining the guests and continuously broke down. The first run of the hotel lasted a meager few weeks before needing to close due to a significant loss of money. When they closed up shop in late January 1947, the tables were in the red $275,000. Siegel made every effort to turn the hotel into a success, including continuing renovations and getting all the good press he could possibly attract. On March 1, 1947, the Flamingo Hotel reopened. Meyer Lansky was present. While the hotel was finally turning a profit, the Mafia bosses were tired of waiting on Siegel.

It was identified that most of the unexpected costs of the construction of the Flamingo Hotel were due to Siegel skimming, misappropriating, and mismanaging funds. Meyer Lansky, once Siegel's partner and close friend on the East Coast, was now a prominent member of the Syndicate and, to say the least, was not very happy with the turn of events. On June 20, 1947, Bugsy Siegel was violently murdered in the home of Virginia Hill. At the same time, three of Lansky's men entered the Flamingo, declaring they were now in charge of the operation. Lansky subsequently denied all involvement, but all signs pointed to a Syndicate-sanctioned hit.

There have also been many theories around why Virginia Hill was not at home during the murder. It has been suggested that she was a cash runner for various Mafia members, including those of the Chicago Outfit. Additionally, leaders like Jack Dragna used her for information on Siegel's activity. When it came time for the execution, Hill was notified to leave town and tell Siegel that she was traveling to France to purchase wine for the Flamingo. Siegel arranged for her to fly on a private jet, unaware that he would soon face his own demise that she knew was coming (*Notable Name: Virginia Hill*, n.d.).

Police completed a rudimentary investigation but stated that there were too many suspects for them to ever be able to isolate one individual. Their only eyewitness was Allen Smiley, the co-owner of the Flamingo Hotel and Casino in Las Vegas. Smiley said the two had gone to dinner, and Siegel had been in high spirits. He said there was no indication from the other man that a hit was expected. There was an open window in the home, allowing the gunmen to fire several shots into the living room. Four met their mark on Bugsy, killing him. One merely ripped Smiley's coat sleeve.

Police Chief C.H. Anderson had assisted in arresting Albert Greenberg in New York for a suspected $114,000 jewelry heist. Upon his arrest, Greenberg provided Siegel as his alibi only to learn of his execution. With that information, he began spilling more details that enlightened Anderson to the potential reasons behind the hit. One of Siegel's men was likely to have sent back information to the New York families that he was committing a double-cross. The Syndicate's primary sources of income came from illegal narcotics trafficking and gambling, and it was suggested that Siegel had established branches of these operations on the West Coast. Additionally, his work with the Flamingo was bringing unwanted publicity to the mob. This likely resulted in the Syndicate telling him he needed to shape up or expect to be taken out of operation. Unfortunately for Siegel, he made the choice to refuse, leading to his demise.

The Battle of Sunset Strip

Sunset Boulevard began in the Plaza district where so much of the Italian family activities were centered. From there, it made its way through the Hollywood and Beverly Hills areas before continuing into the Pacific Coast Highway. The area widely known as the Sunset Strip was a mere 15 blocks of this long road, covering less than 2 miles.

Writing for Esquire in August 1961, Bernard Wolfe states that geographically, the Strip began at Switzer Boulevard, but institutionally it was anchored at Schwab's drug store near Crescent Heights. The western end was considered to be Doheny Road, near the Beverly Hills city limits, where the bridle path once began in the median. (*The Sunset Strip*, 2020)

With the end of Prohibition, it was expected that the Sunset Strip would turn toward legitimate business operations. In fact, these businesses and apartment complexes were rapidly appearing along the 1.7-mile stretch. Instead, as alcohol was decriminalized, a new outlaw era would take hold. "The man responsible for this new, faster Strip was Billy Wilkerson, a knockabout Southerner from Tennessee who had hit pay dirt when he started the influential *The Hollywood Reporter* in 1933" (Meares, 2019). Wilkerson had previously been a part of New York's speakeasy operations. In Hollywood, he owned the Vendome, a high-end delicatessen that also served illegal champagne and imported European liquors. It made for an interesting racket for a man who didn't drink alcohol at all. In January 1934, Wilkerson leased the Café la Boheme. He was originally planning on storing his newly legalized champagne in the location until he was encouraged by several popular movie stars to open an exclusive nightclub. To get things rolling, he blackmailed producer Myron Selznick into throwing the most lavish of grand opening parties. With a remarkable makeover, the location soon became known as the Trocadero. Wilkerson and the Trocadero were known for an air of danger that floated around them, enticing many customers to come in for a closer look. Eventually, Wilkerson would tire of the Trocadero and a mysterious kitchen fire would gut the majority of the building. He moved on to purchase and open Ciro's, a supper club. Through both businesses, he had significant dealings with high-level Mafia members, including Johnny Roselli, Tony Cornero, and Bugsy Siegel. "As *Hollywood Reporter* staffer David Alexander later explained: 'Organized crime came to Hollywood through Billy'" (Meares, 2019).

In the 1920s, gambling was a significant draw for those who visited the Strip. Homer "Slim" Gordon, a prominent figure in organized crime, had opened a gambling den in the home of late actor Wallace Reid in 1929. Amidst the controversy of the kidnapping of bookmaker Zeke Caress in 1930, Les Bruneman managed another gambling club on the Strip. The Clover Club was a casino operated out of a private home by the members of the Spring Street Combination. Later in the 1940s, one of those members, George Goldie, would be the operator of the Trocadero, which was suspected of being an illegal gambling den beneath the surface of legitimate business. Another member of the Combination, Eddie Nealis, also operated his own illicit house gambling on the Strip, "which featured in a notorious robbery involving Betty Grable and other celebrities on New Year's Eve, 1945" (*The Sunset Strip*, 2020).

Overall, the Strip marketed itself as the place to be for daytime and nighttime entertainment, no matter the individual's preferences.

While Siegel was alive and active, his chief lieutenant was Mickey Cohen. Born Meyer Harris Cohen on September 4, 1913, to a poor Brooklyn family, Cohen would grow up in Los Angeles with his five other siblings. During the Prohibition era, his older brothers operated a drug store, which provided him the means of learning how to make bootleg liquor. During this period, he also took up boxing and selling newspapers to earn an income. However, when he turned 15, he ran away from home to become a professional boxer in Cleveland. When the Great Depression began, Cohen was a professional boxer and an enforcer for the Cleveland crime family. He would create trouble in Cleveland, resulting in his transfer to the Chicago Outfit under Al Capone. "He soon began running his own armed robbery crew for the Outfit under Capone's leadership in prison. After an incident involving a savage assault during an armed robbery gone wrong, Cohen was forced to leave Chicago and moved back home to Los Angeles" (*Mickey Cohen*, n.d.). With his newfound partnership with Siegel, the pair would build a successful crime syndicate that involved a horse race wire service, prostitution, labor unions, and narcotics. Throughout the 1940s, they were well known and greatly feared in the Los Angeles community.

Siegel and Cohen were largely credited with bringing order to the "Mickey Mouse Mafia" that Dragna was operating. The local authorities gave the organization that name because they saw it as a poorly organized unit with a severe lack of leadership. However, it was not until several bosses later that the name would be applied with several people incorrectly tying it to Dragna. As Siegel was spending increasingly more time in Las Vegas to focus on the construction of the Flamingo Hotel, Cohen began his climb up the ladder in the underworld by strategically taking out his rivals. At the same time, the Strip began to change with events like the closing of the Trocadero and Clover Club. Cohen established a haberdashery to front all his illegal activities. At this location, it was believed an attempt was made on his life as Harry "Hooky" Rothman was gunned down.

In 1949, the Battle of Sunset Strip occurred. Mickey Cohen was leaving Sherry's Restaurant when shots rang out. At one time, this restaurant had been known as Café Lamaze and was one of the primary influencers in 1935 in transforming the Sunset Strip into the glamorous and alluring location that drew people in. Cohen also survived this attack on his life, but his henchman Edward "Neddie" Herbert, was killed. Just the day before, Attorney General Fred Howser appointed a bodyguard for Cohen. During the shooting, this bodyguard, Harry Cooper, was injured along with Columnist Florabelle Muir and actress Dee David. The police response was to heavily patrol the Sunset Strip in an attempt to eliminate illegal and mobster activity (*The Sunset Strip*, 2020). This wouldn't be the only attempt made on Cohen's life.

Upon Siegel's demise, Cohen immediately assumed control of his rackets. Unlike Siegel, Cohen refused to submit to Dragna's authority. He also began developing his own crime family to rival the Los Angeles crime family. In response, Dragna began recruiting Cohen's new members and killing off others. At the same time, many more hits were attempted on Cohen's life, but he came out alive every time, including when his home was bombed. Eventually, several Los Angeles crime family members would be arrested in connection with that bombing but never charged. It was assumed that the family either committed the bombing or knew who did. The family members arrested included Jack Dragna's brother Tom, his two sons Louis and Frank Paul, and Dragna's son Frank Paul.

Dragna fled California to avoid being questioned by authorities but later turned himself in. While he was missing, authorities conducted an extensive search and were on the verge of believing that harm had come his way. What may be most interesting during his absence is a statement made by Cohen. According to an article in the Tampa Bay Times in 1950, Cohen was reported to have said that Dragna is "one of my closest friends and not a rival of any kind, and as far as I know his only business is importing bananas and olive oil" ("Mob Leader Makes Getaway in California," 1950). Despite his absolute demonstration of omertà, Cohen was also questioned in the incident and was subsequently jailed for tax evasion in 1951. The Los Angeles crime family swooped in on his gambling operations with him out of the picture.

Lasting Legacy

In 1950, Senator Estes Kefauver set out to expose and rid the country of the ever-growing gangster problem. During these hearings, Dragna and many other high-ranking members of the Los Angeles crime family were questioned. He denied all accusations. Despite the challenges made against the family, it remained strong in the face of adversity. These hearings were also held throughout the nation, with some being televised. A crime committee alleged that James Ragen, Sr., the former head of the Continental Press, had declared Dragna the "Al Capone of Los Angeles" as he lay dying.

While there is likely little truth behind this story, as the Chicago Outfit gunned Ragen down to take over the wire service, the moniker stuck.

Later, the California Crime Commission would identify Dragna as a significant force in the criminal underworld. In 1953, he was ordered by the United States Government to be deported for illegal entry into the country. Despite his initial entry being in 1914, the charges were related to a 1932 entry into the United States from Mexico. Dragna went to Mexico for three days and returned across the border without the appropriate documentation. It was this border crossing that the Commission focused on. Dragna never contested that he failed to become a citizen of the country; however, his lawyer vowed to appeal the deportation all the way to the Supreme Court if needed.

Dragna's wife lost her battle with cancer in 1953, and his health also began to decline. These factors made things increasingly difficult for him. With the establishment of Captain Lynn White's Intelligence Division, he faced constant harassment, which impeded his progress of expansion, and the deportation efforts continued. The result was severe negative impacts on his personal lifestyle and gambling operations. His brother had purchased several properties in Las Vegas, but with all the obstacles, including a restrictive order that kept Dragna detained in Los Angeles County, he was never able to see his dream of expanding into Nevada become a reality. He was able to set up a beneficial agreement between the family and the Sheriff's Department. "Also, the federal files reveal the Dragnas received a piece of the action from casino operator Benny Binion, and a wire-tapped telephone conversation strongly suggests Jack Dragna and his associate Allen Smiley had an interest in the Desert Inn with Frank Milano and his Cleveland partners" (Niotta, n.d.).

Dragna died of a heart attack on February 23, 1956, in a hotel in Hollywood, effectively bringing an end to his era of leadership as one of the many bosses to come to the Los Angeles Mafia crime family. Interestingly, many still feared his name in the underworld, crediting him as "the only classic Godfather the city has ever known" (Niotta, n.d.). However, with his death came a decline of the Los Angeles Mafia crime family—or did it?

CHAPTER 3

FRANK DESIMONE TAKES OVER

With the death of Jack Dragna, the Los Angeles crime family needed a new leader. Because he had been the underboss of Dragna, Momo Adamo had expected he would be the next natural choice for succession. However, the family had different plans. Johnny Roselli's name was also put in the pot, and many thought he'd be a shoo-in. In an upset that Roselli believed to be rigged, Frank DeSimone was named the new boss and head of the Los Angeles crime family. DeSimone was once a lawyer who turned to the gangster lifestyle. He was one of only two bosses to have established their careers in this manner. Following his defeat in the vote, Roselli returned to the Chicago Outfit. Because the family chose their new boss, they played a hand in what would become a significant decline in their influence and power.

A Decline in the Los Angeles Family

Throughout the 1950s, many Mafia families were prospering nationwide. Unfortunately for the Los Angeles crime family, there was a significant decline in their power and business transactions following the death of Jack Dragna. In 1950, William H. Parker took on the position of Chief of Police for the Los Angeles Police

Department. With this change in leadership, authorities no longer assisted Mafia activity and instead began cracking down harshly on it. Due to its significantly weakened status without Dragna, the family steadily lost ground to the Chicago Outfit and the New York families as they began expanding their own hold in California. Many of these Mafia members were making the move out west to establish a foothold in the labor racketeering sector where there had previously been no movement. Additionally, many moved to California before making their way to Las Vegas.

The Gangster Squad was a special task force developed by the Los Angeles Police Department in response to 50 unsolved gangland murders that occurred over the course of the first half of the 20th century. It would later be known as the Organized Crime Intelligence Division (OCID). The task force was created in 1946 by the current police chief, Clemence B. Horrall. Initially, it was a group of eight agents who were tasked with battling the organized crime threat in Los Angeles and spying on potentially corrupt officers. Based on laws today, the Gangster Squad used many means that would have resulted in the agents losing their badges. LAPD Chief William Whorton bulked up the team in 1949 and renamed it OCID. In 1950, when William Parker became the police chief, he further expanded the team, adding a female field team. While Dragna was still alive, this task force harassed the Los Angeles crime family and Mickey Cohen's family. This continued throughout the 1950s.

When Dragna was found dead in his hotel room in 1956, the family moved to elect its new leader. In a stunning upset that some believed to have been rigged, Frank DeSimone was announced as the next boss of the Los Angeles crime family. But who was this man, and how effective was he at leading the family?

Frank DeSimone

Frank DeSimone was the son of the Los Angeles crime family's former don, Rosario DeSimone. He was born in 1909 in Pueblo, Colorado. In his younger years, the DeSimone family relocated to Southern California. He had several familial ties to the Mafia, including Simone Scozzari and Joseph Civello. His nephew, Thomas DeSimone, was one of the enforcers for the New York City-based Lucchese crime family. When he grew up, he attended and graduated from the University of Southern California Law School, becoming a lawyer in May 1933. Following the passing of the bar, DeSimone also became enmeshed in mob business. He was part of one of the many failed attempts on Mickey Cohen's life. Because he had a reputable job as a respected attorney, DeSimone was generally able to avoid serious scrutiny from law enforcement.

In the 1940s and 1950s, he served as legal counsel to several important members of the Los Angeles crime family, including Jimmy Fratianno and Johnny Roselli. When DeSimone was elected as the new boss, Roselli was not the only member to leave the family for the Chicago Outfit. Fratianno was in prison at the time of the appointment but also believed it was a rigged outcome. When he was released from prison in 1960, he also made his way to the Windy City.

With Dragna's passing, Tom Dragna also retired from the family. This move further weakened the organization. It was quickly discovered that DeSimone was not a great leader, with many considering him incompetent. His reign was also surrounded by controversy. According to an informant, DeSimone was accused of raping former underboss Momo Adamo's wife. As a result of this incident, Adamo attempted a murder-suicide by shooting his wife and then himself. However, while Adamo died, his wife survived. With Adamo's death, the family was in severe turmoil, missing the boss, underboss, and consigliere of the Dragna era.

One of the first acts DeSimone performed as the leader of the Los Angeles crime family was to attend the Apalachin Meeting of 1957, a large gathering of mob members. Accompanying him was his underboss, Simone Scozzari. While DeSimone had previously had a reputation for being a straitlaced lawyer, that would all change at this meeting. The police raided the event and ousted him as a mobster. "DeSimone was sentenced to four years for conspiracy to obstruct justice as a result of the Apalachin meeting but never served prison time due to a reversal of his conviction" (Younger, 1978). Additionally, Scozzari became a significant person of interest and was eventually deported as an illegal immigrant in 1962.

Ruining Reputations

DeSimone was credited with ruining the reputation of the Los Angeles crime family. Despite this, *Look Magazine* published a feature article touting him as one of the most notable organized crime members of the current decade. His response was to sue the magazine. Jimmy Fratianno also held DeSimone responsible for his time served in prison. In 1953, Fratianno's extortion case was sent to Folsom Prison for a six-year sentence. He also accused DeSimone of failing to represent him correctly in his defense because of the failure to record one of the key witnesses. This witness skipped town before ever taking the stand, leaving Fratianno high and dry during his trial. Eventually, DeSimone would be disbarred due to his connections to organized crime.

The family also received more negative publicity with the death of soldier John Stompanato, Jr. He was in a relationship with actress Lana Turner when he was killed. According to Turner and her daughter, Stompanato had a violent streak when things weren't going according to his wishes. On April 4, 1958, he was allegedly beating Turner. Her daughter proceeded to stab him in the midsection with a kitchen knife, resulting in his death. A heavily publicized trial ended in a not-guilty verdict because it was labeled a justifiable homicide.

While many relate the Mickey Mouse Mafia title with Dragna, the truth behind the name is that it came from bosses down the line, starting with DeSimone. Dragna has been recognized as being significantly more successful than the other bosses who followed in his wake, eliminating the problem of Los Angeles being open game for all Mafia activity.

Plotting the Death of DeSimone

It was estimated that the remaining family in Los Angeles only numbered around 30 in 1965. However, their presence was strong in San Diego. DeSimone feared having the family participate in shakedowns of the local independent bookmakers and gamblers. He believed these individuals would simply run to the police, bringing more problems to the family. However, this fear would lead to more problems for the boss.

In the 1960s, Joseph Bonanno hatched a plan to overthrow the Commission leaders. He orchestrated a murder plan that would take out the top Mafia bosses, Carlo Gambino, Thomas Lucchese, and Stefano Magaddino. Because DeSimone failed to fully exploit all the criminal opportunities that Los Angeles afforded him and the family, Bonanno added him to the list. Fortunately for DeSimone, the plan was thwarted. He never learned about it until well after the fact, but it made him paranoid for the remainder of his life.

DeSimone spent the final years of his life living in Downey, California, with his elderly mother. He never went out at night. He died on August 4, 1967, from a heart attack at the age of 58, ending his very unsuccessful reign as boss of the Los Angeles crime family.

CHAPTER 4

NICOLO LICATA'S RISE TO POWER

With the death of Frank DeSimone, the Los Angeles crime family faced even more turmoil and disorganization. Due to his ineffectiveness as a leader, his successor was set up with a challenge from the start. Additionally, local and federal law enforcement began cracking down even harder on organized crime nationwide, making it harder for the family to operate their business as they once had. With the new boss, Nicolo "Nick" Licata, in position, the family would hold onto its precarious position in Los Angeles but would not see the success it once had under Jack Dragna.

Old Man Nick Licata

Nicolo Licata was born in Camporeale, Sicily, on February 20, 1897. Camporeale was a small town located in the Palermo province. However, the surname Licata also implies he may have had familial connections in Licata, a city located in the lower area of Sicily. His parents were Calogera and Vita, who also had six other sons and two daughters. At 16, he took the voyage from Palermo to Ellis Island on the Sant' Anna with $25 in his pocket. He arrived on December 5, 1913. At that time, he proceeded to Brooklyn to join his brother Leonardo. While in the United States, he anglicized his name from Nicolo to Nick. The first place Licata settled was in Detroit. While living there, he met and married his wife, Josephine. They had two children while living in Highland Park, Michigan.

In the 1920s, Licata would find the bootlegging industry to be a lucrative operation. He took part in these covert dealings throughout the Prohibition era. Eventually, he would become a made man in Detroit's crime family. At one point, Licata offended the crime boss, Joseph Zerilli, which led to his relocation to Los Angeles in 1929. Once there, he became close with Jack Dragna, who convinced Zerilli to cancel the contract he placed on Licata's life for the infraction. The Los Angeles crime family accepted him with open arms, making him a full-fledged member. Licata and then-consigliere Tom Dragna developed a close relationship. Licata was naturalized on March 25, 1932.

When Licata first relocated to California, he was initially a grocer. He would later become a cafe owner in Burbank for a business known as the Five O'Clock Cafe. He also owned several barrooms while operating as a bookmaker and loan shark. In 1945, he was arrested on charges of refilling liquor containers. "Licata earned notice in the underworld through the summer 1951 murders of Kansas City Mafiosi Tony Brancato and Tony Trombino" (Hunt, n.d.-c). Brancato and Trombino, also known as the Two Tonys, were muscling in on the Los Angeles crime family's rackets as the Kansas City crime family attempted to make a westward push on its enterprises. In mid-August of that year, police detained and questioned several key figures, including Sam Lazes, Sam London, and Jimmy and Warren Fratianno. They were also seeking Charles Battaglia and Angelo Polizzi, who were currently missing in action.

While Jimmy Fratianno was a prime suspect in the slayings, Licata was his alibi. That night, Licata had held a fish fry at his Burbank restaurant, the Five O'Clock Club. Several of the guests and one waitress testified that Fratianno was present the entire evening when the murders were happening. While all those in question were arrested, the Los Angeles Police Department could never make a single charge stick. It wasn't until Fratianno became an informant for the Federal Bureau of Investigations (FBI) around 25 years later that their suspicions were confirmed. During this period, Nick Licata was a soldier in the Los Angeles crime family.

In 1952, Dragna made the decision to advance Jimmy Fratianno through the ranks, making him a caporegime. However, it was believed that Licata was the more logical choice for the promotion. To pacify Licata once this decision had been made, Dragna allowed him to work in an elevated position. While working directly underneath Dragna, Licata made beneficial connections with the New Orleans, Dallas, Kansas City, and Detroit Mafia families. At the time of Dragna's death in 1956, then-boss Frank DeSimone named Nick Licata as his consigliere, a heavily supported choice by the family's younger members. When underboss Simone Scozzari was deported in 1962, Licata was promoted to fill the open position. He was promoted again in 1967 following DeSimone's death without any opposition. However, when he became the boss of the family, there were clear signs of division among the ranks.

Around that time, the Los Angeles Police Department had gained a significant amount of information about the family. In 1967, top Los Angeles crime family hitman Frank Bompensiero became a key informant, working undercover for law enforcement. Before that, in 1963, Joe Valachi, a member of the Genovese crime family, outed the Mafia as a secret, powerful criminal organization and identified Licata as a high-ranking member of the Los Angeles family. As a result, the Los Angeles Police Department and FBI proceeded to hound Licata. In addition to the stress these hassles caused, he was never truly able to solidify the power of the family under his wing. There is some indication that Jack Dragna's son took over a branch of the organization shortly after Licata's rise to the top, further separating the ranks (Hunt, n.d.-c). Additionally, with previous interactions with the Kansas City family, he was able to convince their members to remain out of Los Angeles. However, he faced problems with the Cleveland family attempting to infiltrate his operations.

Licata's underboss was Joseph Dippolito, commonly known in the underworld as Joe Dip. He was born in Brooklyn on December 28, 1914. His parents were Salvatore Charles (Charlie) and Angelina Dippolito. He served one year in prison during Prohibition for a felony charge after being caught illegally transporting liquor. When he was released, he relocated from New York to Fontana, California, located near San Bernardino, to join his parents. During the Great Depression, the Dippolito family purchased diamonds from sellers in Los Angeles, Ontario, and New York at discounted rates. They were eventually able to make a significant profit off those jewels. Joe and Charlie were soon successful owners of several businesses in Rancho Cucamonga, including a hotel, a liquor and market store, and several vineyards. They became prominent faces in the Inland Empire and were involved in several major real estate deals.

Joe Dippolito had made a name for himself in the Los Angeles crime family as a powerful and effective killer and hitman. In September 1949, he helped Jimmy Fratianno carry out a hit on Mickey Cohen's loyalist Frank Niccoli. The body was then buried in Dippolito's vineyard in Rancho Cucamonga with a sack of lye. This location would become a popular burial ground for Los Angeles Mafia murder victims.

Jack Dragna inducted him into the family in 1952, when he started as a soldier under Jimmy Fratianno. His father, Charlie, was also a made man in the family and had been inducted five years previously. Seeing his worth, when he became boss, Licata chose to promote Dippolito to the position of underboss.

On January 31, 1969, Joe Dippolito was brought to trial for three counts of lying under oath in relation to a case from the previous year. He was accused of providing false statements in an inquiry made on May 6, 1968, he was accused of providing false statements about a liquor license. Released on $10,000 bail, he was scheduled for arraignment. On May 17, 1969, two of the three charges stuck with a conviction and sentencing of five years apiece. He was released on a $10,000 bond to await the appeal of this conviction. During this time, he was recognized as Licata's underboss. Judge Warren J. Ferguson reduced the sentence by half on April 16, 1971, leaving Joe Dip to only serve five years. However, on December 13, 1971, he was paroled after serving only eight months of the sentence. "Joe Dip was released from prison after San Bernardino mayor Al C. Ballard, Police Chief Louis J. Fortuna, and California Superior Court Judge Joseph A. Katz vouched for Dippolito in glowing letters written in 1969 to a probation officer" (*Joseph Dippolito*, 2023).

On January 14, 1974, Dippolito died from a heart attack while attending his daughter Josephine's wedding. Three months earlier, he had been hospitalized due to a heart condition and had remained in poor health. He was buried at the Bellevue Cemetery and Mausoleum.

Licata Is Called to the Grand Jury

On January 10, 1969, Julius Anthony Petro of Cleveland was murdered. His car was found at the Los Angeles International Airport with his dead body inside—he had been shot to death. Petro had been a known bank robber. He was also suspected of committing several murders in Cleveland. In July that same year, Nick Licata was called to testify before the Supreme Court about Petro's murder.

During the court session before a federal grand jury, Licata was questioned regarding the structure of the Los Angeles crime syndicate. Holding true to the law of omertà, Licata refused to answer any questions, despite being given immunity by the prosecution. Judge Jesse W. Curtis, Jr. held Licata in contempt of court. The questions related back to the 1957 Apalachin Mafia meeting in New York. Additionally, Judge Curtis questioned whether Licata had replaced Frank DeSimone as the boss of the Los Angeles crime family.

When the judge pressed him for answers, Licata responded, "Your Honor, I stand on the 1st, 4th, 5th, and 6th amendments, which every citizen has a right to do" ("Alleged L.A. Mafia Chief Goes to

Jail," 1969). He was reminded that he could not incriminate himself by answering any questions, to which Licata responded that he didn't feel like answering any of the judge's questions. In a later statement, as he issued a $2,500 bond for Licata, Curtis acknowledged that the Mafia boss would never answer any of the questions as it would result in his death due to the nature of the organization ("Nick Licata Released on $2,500 Bond," 1970). Ultimately, Licata would serve six months in prison for failing to answer the questions asked.

Licata's Life and Death

In the mid-1970s, the family faced several indictments that threatened the freedom of most of the remaining working members. Seven members were arrested in March 1973 for their hand in running an illegal gambling operation in Los Angeles. The business brought in around $250,000 per month in revenue. The key witness for the prosecution was a former Mafia associate, John Dubcek, who turned to being an informant. However, the trial was put on hold when he was gunned down in Las Vegas. This scared many other informants out of testifying. Regardless, the seven men were still convicted. However, they only received light sentences. "Four months later, another 12 men were indicted for conspiracy, racketeering, and extortion against bookmakers, loan sharks, and pornographers" (*Los Angeles Crime Family*, 2023). At this point, Dippolito still had a significant influence throughout San Bernardino and the Inland Empire with a combination of legitimate businesses and criminal enterprises. Because of his reputation and position as underboss, he was seen as the clear option for succession when Licata's time came. However, with his unexpected death coming before the boss's, a new underboss had to be named. His replacement would be Dominic "Jimmy" Brooklier.

Licata retained the formal title of boss but likely didn't have the power that was needed to back it up. The family and territory were essentially in shambles throughout the end of his reign. However, he was able to regain a respectable standing with the Detroit Mafia family. His son, Carlo, married William "Black Bill" Tocco's daughter, Grace. Tocco was the underboss of the Detroit family at the time of the marriage. Licata made the trip to attend the wedding in Detroit. Officer Jack O'Mara located the wedding invitations as he carried out an arrest warrant for Licata. He illegally seized the invitations in a transparent demonstration of law enforcement's desperation to take down organized crime in the state. During the 1960s and 1970s, Frank Stellino spent time as an active member of the Mafia in Los Angeles, keeping things in the literal family, as he was Licata's son-in-law.

While battling the illness that would end his life, Nick Licata passed his final days in Santa Monica at Saint John's Health Center. He died nine months after Dippolito on October 19, 1974. On October 23, a Requiem Mass was held in his honor at St. Peter's Roman Catholic Church before he was buried at the Holy Cross Cemetery. Around 150 people were in attendance.

While the Los Angeles crime family was not as strong as it once was, the next successor, Dominic Brooklier, was able to stabilize the business. However, with his reign came significant damage.

CHAPTER 5
THE BROOKLIER DECADE

After the death of Nick Licata, his second underboss, Dominic Brooklier, would take over the head of the Los Angeles crime family. In the beginning, Brooklier would see significant success at stabilizing the business operations that had previously been spiraling out of control. However, with several key members of the family turning into FBI informants, he dealt with significant damage. His reign over the family extended through the mid-1970s, with his primary income sources coming from extortion, gambling, and pornography. Ultimately, it would be another example of an unsuccessful leadership of the Los Angeles crime family; however, this time, it was due to the turncoats within the family, not because of the leader himself.

Reigning Brooklier

Dominic Phillip Brooklier was born on November 19, 1914. His birth name was Domenico Brucceleri, but he also went by the name Jimmy Regace. Brooklier's original entry into the world of the Mafia was with Mickey Cohen. Using the name Regace, he joined Cohen's gambling operations in the 1940s. When the Sunset Wars rolled around, Brooklier quickly defected, joining the ranks of Jack

Dragna's family. On the side of the Los Angeles crime family, he took part in the numerous attempts on Cohen's life, including one where he was the incompetent triggerman. "His chief claim to fame as a hitman in that struggle was attempting to shotgun Cohen as he came out of a restaurant. Just as Brooklier, accompanied by another gunman, squeezed the trigger, Cohen noticed a tiny scratch on the fender of his new Cadillac and bent down to inspect it, thereby avoiding a fatal hit" (Sifakis, 2010).

Between 1947 and 1953, Brooklier worked heavily with Jimmy Fratianno in the loan sharking business. Loan sharks provide loans to borrowers outside of the laws and regulations of banking systems. Their interest rates are incredibly high, and they have stringent collection policies. They generally use blackmail, violence, and coercion practices to collect on their borrowers' debts.

In the late 1960s, Brooklier was elevated to a caporegime. He was given territory and a crew in Orange County, where he was also living at the time. Caporegime is the formal name for a capo or captain within the ranks of a Mafia and is the position above the soldiers and beneath the underboss. Sometime after, he completed a legal name change to officially become Dominic Brooklier on paper.

In early 1974, Brooklier was promoted again to the position of underboss under Nick Licata. His time as Joe Dippolitto's replacement was short-lived, as Licata's death came just a few months later. The family chose to elect Brooklier as the next boss of the Los Angeles crime family. During his reign, he was able to make money for the family through various means, including pornography, extortion, and drugs. However, the independent bookmaking rackets always remained just out of his reach. "The Los Angeles family would shake down movie producers in the porn industry. These producers would then pay a fee to their Mafia backers, usually on the East Coast, to set things straight with the L.A. mob" (*Los Angeles Crime Family*, 2023). These movie producers didn't know that the East Coast Mafia backers would turn around and split that money with the Los Angeles crime family.

Death Ordered to Frank Bompensiero

As one of Brooklier's acts as the boss of the Los Angeles crime family, he would later order the death of Frank Bompensiero due to the hitman's growing criticisms of the family and insurmountable evidence that he was participating with the FBI. Bompensiero was born on October 29, 1905, in Milwaukee. His family immigrated to the United States from Porticello, Sicily in 1904. They traveled with the Balistrieri family. Later, Frank Balistrieri would be the head of the Milwaukee crime family.

While Bompensiero was a child, he attended Andrew Jackson Elementary School until he dropped out in the third grade. His primary job while living in Milwaukee was at an automotive parts manufacturer. He eventually relocated to San Diego in the mid-1920s. During this period, Frank Bompensiero was initiated into the realm of organized crime when he began a bootlegging operation with liquor coming over the border from Tijuana. He later married Thelma Jan San-Felippe, and the two had a daughter named Anna, who would give them a grandson, Frank. Their first home was in El Cerrito, but they later relocated to Pacific Beach.

Bompensiero was active in the United States Army between 1942 and 1943 during World War II.

Early in his time in San Diego during the 1920s, Bompensiero met and developed a close relationship with Jack Dragna. Bompensiero's allure came from his fearlessness, which led Dragna to become his mentor. Over the years, he faced several arrests for crimes, including a liquor violation, firearms possession, kidnapping, murder, and illegal gambling. However, most of the charges were dropped. He would later serve one year, starting in 1932, in prison at the McNeil Island Corrections Center for the liquor charge.

Dragna quickly became impressed with Bompensiero, making him a caporegime and placing him over the Los Angeles crime family's interests in San Diego. "Wanted for questioning in the Redondo Beach murder of mobster Les Brunemann, Frank Bompensiero left California but was able to return in 1941 after an innocent man was convicted of Brunemann's murder" (*Frank Bompensiero*, 2023). Throughout the 1940s and 1950s, he was quite a businessman. He owned the Gold Rail Cafe in the U.S. Grant Hotel, a music store, and a horseracing wire service company. His business ventures included partnerships with Gaspare Matranga and Tom Dragna's son and nephew. The Bompensiero crew also operated several bars in the San Diego area where they conducted their loan sharking business.

He was recognized by Jack Dragna as a true shakedown artist and a superior hitman. Bompensiero also made one of the infamous failed attempts on Mickey Cohen's life and is credited with killing Neddie Herbert of the Cohen gang. His crew in San Diego "included Tony

Mirabile, Paul Mirabile, Gaspare Matranga, Joe Adamo, Biaggio Bonventre, and Joseph Li Mandri" (*Frank Bompensiero*, 2023). When it came to Los Angeles, he kept very close ties with Jimmy "The Weasel" Fratianno and Leo "Lips" Moceri. On several occasions, these two were his partners on mob-sanctioned hits.

Later, in 1955, his luck ran out when dealing with an illegal liquor license transaction. He was convicted of bribery and conspiracy in relation to the transaction and was sentenced to prison. His sentence started at the California Institution for Men (CIM), often called Chino, located in Chino, California. During his incarceration, his wife passed away from a stroke. Bompensiero was given a police escort to the funeral. "He was later transferred to San Quentin State Prison in Northern California, the same prison where Jimmy Fratianno was serving a prison sentence for extortion" (*Frank Bompensiero*, 2023).

While in prison, he would face another significant loss—Jack Dragna would die of a heart attack, leaving Frank DeSimone to be elected the new boss. As one of his first acts as boss, DeSimone demoted Bompensiero from caporegime down to soldier. To replace him, he promoted Tony Mirabile as the new head of family operations in San Diego. Bompensiero was utterly outraged at this action and attempted to transfer to the Chicago Outfit. However, he was blocked. Johnny Roselli later revealed that he didn't want Bompensiero and Fratianno to leave Los Angeles for Chicago, as it would leave a bad impression. The other Mafias might get the impression that all good workers wanted out of the Los Angeles crime family. Bompensiero proceeded to work for several friends and associates to complete the requirements of his parole.

Shortly after his prison release, Bompensiero developed several business ventures in Las Vegas. His dealings involved Moe Dalitz, the Cleveland mobster and casino owner, and Anthony Spilotro of the Chicago Outfit. He also worked closely with Joseph Bonanno in Arizona. Bonanno was the retired head of the Bonanno crime family. At one time, he also counted John Roselli as an ally until the two had a falling out over a hit dispute. Then, in 1967, Bompensiero and Fratianno were arrested over a union scheme tied to the Fratianno Trucking Company. Fratianno's company was accused of violating PUC regulations. While in El Centro Jail with an extremely high bail, Bompensiero felt immeasurable pressure. As a result, he became an FBI informant, and the charges against him were dropped.

In the 1970s, he teamed up with Tony Spilotro in Las Vegas to run a loan sharking operation. The pair also worked together in 1975 to commit a murder. Tamara Rand was a multimillion-dollar real estate broker and investor who was suing the mob's frontman in Las Vegas, Allen Glick. She had loaned him $2 million and was attempting to get the money back. With Bompensiero as the getaway driver, Spilotro snuck into her home and fatally shot her.

While Bompensiero was active in the Los Angeles crime family following the death of Jack Dragna, he was highly critical of its leadership. By the time Dominic Brooklier took over, he had heard enough of the criticism and made the fateful decision to have Bompensiero murdered. However, Bompensiero was a very careful man, resulting in the task being very challenging to complete. In a ruse to make him more comfortable and less cautious, Brooklier promoted him to consigliere in 1976. Despite this move, the family was still attempting to kill him six months later.

The FBI used Bompensiero again in 1977 when they set up a sting operation. They used a front pornography operation called Forex and had him convince the family to extort money from it. The sting was a success, and when the family found out about it, Fratianno immediately suspected Bompensiero of being an informant. On February 10, 1977, Frank Bompensiero was finally taken out. He "was shot to death at close range with a silenced .22 caliber handgun while walking home after using a pay phone outside an Arco Station in the Pacific Beach neighborhood of San Diego" (*Frank Bompensiero*, 2023). It was revealed in 1978 by Jimmy Fratianno that Los Angeles crime family member Thomas Ricciardi committed the murder in exchange for entry into the ranks of the family. Jack LoCicero was said to have been waiting in the getaway car. Law enforcement later charged Ricciardi with the murder; however, he would die before the trial could begin. All other defendants were acquitted of murder but were charged with racketeering.

Love-Hate Relationship

Aladena James "Jimmy The Weasel" Fratianno was born November 14, 1913, in Naples, Italy. His family would later immigrate to the United States, making their home near Cleveland, Ohio. Fratianno's life of crime would start at a young age, as he was arrested on suspicion of rape at 19. However, he would never be formally charged with the crime. At 21, he faced robbery charges only to be acquitted. Then in 1937, he again faced robbery charges, but this time, he was found guilty and sent to prison for more than seven years. When he was paroled in 1945, he moved to California, where he became involved with Mickey Cohen.

Eventually, Fratianno would become part of the Los Angeles crime family until his departure for the Chicago Outfit in 1960, following what he believed to be a rigged election for the position of boss. He would eventually return at the request of Tom Dragna in 1975 while the family was in need of a leader. At that time, Dominic Brooklier and his underboss Samuel Sciortini were given what would be a 20-month prison sentence. Dragna and Fratianno were named co-acting bosses. Fratianno spent the time traveling across the country, creating new deals and building new connections. His goal was to rebuild the ailing family, regaining the respect of the other Mafia families. Fratianno wanted to make a name for himself to be considered the logical choice for boss even after Brooklier's return from prison. However, Brooklier was immediately put back into position as boss upon his return, placing Fratianno back into the lowly position of soldier.

While he was acting boss, Tom Dragna approached Jimmy Fratianno about the need to have Frank Bompensiero killed. Bompensiero and Fratianno had a long history of friendship and trust, which made this request very upsetting for him. Additionally, it led him to believe that the offer to become acting boss had been a trick to get him to return to the Los Angeles crime family. Brooklier assumed that because of their close ties, Fratianno could easily trick Bompensiero into a situation where he would be easily taken out. Instead, Fratianno stalled until the family elected to give the hit to another family member.

In 1977, the love-hate relationship between Brooklier and Fratianno began to sour even further. The boss had Fratianno attend a sit-down where he accused the soldier of running his own crew in Los Angeles. Additionally, Brooklier accused him of badmouthing the family and its leadership, just like Bompensiero. Based on the things said in the conversation, Fratianno suspected that the goal was to slander his reputation and set him up to be murdered. Ultimately, Brooklier would issue that hit because he felt Fratianno was misrepresenting himself and was likely an informant. However, he would need help to see it through and would end up asking the Chicago Outfit for assistance. This move would make it clear that the Los Angeles crime family was a shell of what it once was, as it could no longer take care of its own problematic members. Additionally, this opened the door for opportunistic members of the Chicago family to make their move on a weakened Los Angeles.

Another Hit to the Los Angeles Family

"The fall of the Los Angeles family came when Fratianno became the second American Mafioso to turn state's evidence and testify against the Mafia in court" (*Los Angeles Crime Family*, 2023). It all started to go downhill when Danny Green, an Irish mob boss and FBI informant, was taken out by a car bomb on October 6, 1977. He was known for being an archenemy of the Cleveland crime family, and an eyewitness sketch brought about the arrest of a soldier from the Cleveland crime family, Ray Ferrito. When police searched Ferrito's home, they found evidence that secured the conviction. With the knowledge of Ferrito's arrest, James Licavoli, Mafia boss of the Cleveland family, ordered a hit on his life. This caused Ferrito to testify against his co-conspirators in his 1978 trial. "The

Cuyahoga County District Attorney indicted Licavoli, Angelo Lonardo, Ferritto, Ronald Carabbia and 15 other members of the Cleveland crime family for conspiring towards Danny Greene's murder" (*Los Angeles Crime Family*, 2023). Ferrito also named Jimmy Fratianno as part of the crime, resulting in him being indicted for the bombing. Fratianno also feared for his safety and became a government witness.

Fratianno provided his testimony and, in exchange, pleaded guilty to several murder charges. He was sentenced to 5 years in prison but only served 21 months. He entered the federal Witness Protection Program in 1980 following his testimony that led to five high-level Mafia personnel receiving racketeering convictions. Fratianno published two books about his life, revealing that the Mafia had a $100,000 contract for his murder. However, due to the books being ghostwritten, Fratianno alleged that he never read them nor was he familiar with their content. In 1987, the government removed the Fratiannos from witness protection due to how much money they were costing the program. In approximately ten years, the family cost the government over $1 million. Jimmy Fratianno died of natural causes at his home on June 29, 1993.

Later Charges and Imprisonment

While Brooklier took over the role of family boss in 1974, he would spend most of his time running the operation from behind bars. Over the years, he was convicted on many counts, including "armed robbery, larceny and interstate transportation of forged documents" (Hunt, n.d.-a). He would face jail time in 1975 for extorting funds from those in the gambling and pornography industries. In 1980, Brooklier faced the trial for Frank Bompensiero's murder with Samuel Sciortino and Tom Louis Dragna. The three were acquitted of the murder charges but faced imprisonment for racketeering, conspiracy, and extortion. Jack LoCicero and Michael Rizzitello were also convicted on those same charges.

Brooklier attempted legal appeals for his convictions and remained free during the process. However, he began his four-year federal prison sentence on August 27, 1983. He was initially ordered to serve his time in a Minnesota state prison, but the family convinced the court to assign him to an Arizona prison for health reasons. "Brooklier died in the Federal Metropolitan Correctional Center in Tucson, AZ, on July 18, 1984" (Hunt, n.d.-a). He had suffered a heart attack.

While he was able to keep the family operating from inside his prison cell, his death would ultimately put an end to Brooklier's reign. During his prison time, caporegime Peter Milano helped to run the family on the outside. He would become the next boss of the family.

CHAPTER 6

THE MILANO BROTHERS

With the passing of Brooklier in 1984, the Los Angeles crime family appointed Peter John Milano as its new boss. He would, in turn, select his brother, Carmen "Flipper" Milano, as his underboss. Milano would induct several new members with the intention of rejuvenating the failing family. The Milano brothers were not unlike the leaders of the past in that they faced many problems with law enforcement. Additionally, with informants in their midst, after rebuilding the family, they would face dramatic difficulties and severe limitations on keeping the organization a strong force in the city of Los Angeles.

Peter and Carmen Milano

Peter Milano was born on December 22, 1925, to Anthony and Josephine Milano in Cleveland, Ohio. Anthony Milano may have been the original inspiration for Milano's eventual entrance to organized crime, as he was the underboss of the Cleveland crime family. He held the position from the 1930s until his eventual retirement in 1976. Additionally, his uncle, Frank Milano, held the position of boss for the Cleveland crime family from the early 1930s until 1935. At that time, he fled the country to Mexico to avoid a tax evasion indictment.

As with many crime families, the Cleveland crime family saw its fair share of changes over the years. The family was started by the Lonardo brothers, with the oldest brother, Joseph, as the boss. Tensions quickly rose between the Lonardos and Porrellos. Ultimately, the Porellos would take out Joseph and his son and establish control of the family until the 1930s, when Frank Milano and his gang would muscle into their territory, taking over. He joined the National Crime Syndicate in 1931 and was considered one of the top Mafia bosses nationwide by 1932. The reins of power were quickly handed off to the next leader in 1935 when Frank Milano fled the country.

Peter Milano had other family members involved in organized crime, including his brothers. Initially, his brother Carmen would remain on the straight and narrow as a lawyer. However, he, too, would join the ranks of the Mafia in the 1980s. Peter was also related to John Nardi through marriage. Nardi was a Mafia associate who was killed during the war between Danny Greene and the Cleveland crime family when he defected to the side of the Irish mob. At some point during the 1930s or 1940s, Peter Milano relocated to Beverly Hills, California, with his family. He finished high school and joined the ranks of Mickey Cohen's crime syndicate, focusing on illicit gambling.

Eventually, Peter Milano switched his allegiance from Cohen's gang to the Los Angeles crime family. They would induct him as a made man in 1970. Not long after being made an official soldier, he was promoted to caporegime. While his father was a vital figure in the

Cleveland crime family, he also had significant interests on the West Coast and connections with the Los Angeles crime family.

"In March 1973, Milano and six others were charged with running a rigged gambling operation in Los Angeles that brought in up to $250,000 a month. Their trial was delayed when the key informant and witness, former Mafia associate John Dubcek, was shot and killed in Las Vegas" (*Peter Milano*, 2023). Dubcek's murder may have delayed the trial but didn't stop it from progressing. Other informants became too scared to testify, but this didn't prevent Milano from facing a four-year prison sentence. This operation used prostitutes to lure their customers to the gambling house, which rotated to avoid attracting law enforcement notice. Available games were craps and blackjack, which were illegal to play in California. The operators used rigged equipment, including a crooked wheel, marked cards, and loaded dice to ensure they could take the gamblers for all they had. The family members implicated in the crimes were Peter Milano, Martin C. Calaway, Luigi Gelfuso, John Joseph Vaccaro, Jr., Tony Endreola, and Santo Albert Manfre. Harry P. Coloduros was also implicated, but his involvement is unknown, as he turned state's evidence to implicate the others. Milano, Gelfuso, and Calaway were ultimately convicted by the jury.

A few months later, Peter Milano and 11 others "were indicted for conspiracy, racketeering and extortion against bookmakers, loan sharks, and pornographers" (*Peter Milano*, 2023). He would serve four years on both charges.

In 1981, the Los Angeles crime family faced a significant hit to its structure when several top leaders, including then-boss Dominic

Brooklier, were sentenced to time in prison for racketeering charges. Due to the ensuing power vacuum, Peter Milano stepped up and became the acting boss. When Brooklier died in 1984, the family officially made Milano the boss, and he named his brother, Carmen, the underboss.

Carmen Milano was born on July 27, 1929. In addition to Peter, his brothers included John and Frank Milano. He joined his family in relocating to Beverly Hills around the end of the 1930s and the beginning of the 1940s. As Peter was joining Mickey Cohen's syndicate, Carmen would make a much different choice for his own life. He chose to attend Loyola Marymount University after graduating from high school. After successfully completing his degree program, he was accepted into Loyola Law School. He even joined the Phi Delta Phi fraternity. On January 5, 1955, he passed the bar and officially became a lawyer in the state of California. He then moved back to Cleveland in pursuit of a legal career. "During the 1970s, Milano was paid a retainer for few, if any, legal services to Teamsters Local 410 and 436, which are labor unions that were allegedly controlled by Milano's father" (*Carmen Milano*, 2023). Due to his involvement with fraudulent workers' compensation claims, Carmen Milano was eventually disbarred.

In 1984, when Peter Milano was head of the Los Angeles crime family, Carmen Milano relocated back to California. Before owning his own home, he briefly lived with Caporegime Luigi "Louie" Gelfuso. Not long after moving back to California, Carmen became a made man and named Peter's underboss. His primary job as underboss was to protect Peter from the lower ranks, which would, in turn, shield him from police scrutiny. Carmen also brought the family connections to the Cleveland crime family and several East Coast bosses. He was described as being the tougher of the brothers.

New Members Inducted

One of the first things Peter Milano did as the new boss of the Los Angeles crime family was to induct new members to bulk up the dwindling ranks. These new members included Stephen "Steve the Whale" Cino, singer Charles "Bobby Milano" Caci, Luigi "Louie" Gelfuso Jr. and shylock brothers Lawrence and Anthony 'The Animal Fiato (*Los Angeles Crime Family*, 2023). Kenny Gallo, a one-time mobster who turned informant, credited the Fiato brothers with aiding Milano in rebuilding the family.

With these new members in place, Peter Milano was able to extract mob tax payments to the Los Angeles crime family from almost every bookmaker in the city. Additionally, Anthony Fiato received a loan from Robert "Puggy" Zeichick for $1 million to finance a sizable loan sharking operation. With this move, the family established itself as the dominant force in the loan sharking business in the Los Angeles area. By this time, "the family's influence stretched all the way to Las Vegas, where they had long-standing ties to what the Mafia considered an 'open city' where any family could work" (*Los Angeles Crime Family*, 2023).

1984 Arrest

"Milano was among 20 reputed organized crime figures arrested in 1984, in what law enforcement officials said was a bid to take over a $1 million-a-week bookmaking operation in Los Angeles. Neither of the Milano brothers (nor six of the others originally arrested) were charged due to lack of evidence" (*Carmen Milano*, 2023). However, this would only be the beginning of the Milano brothers' legal problems.

On May 21, 1987, the Los Angeles crime family's entire hierarchy would face various charges in relation to violating the Racketeer Influenced and Corrupt Organizations (RICO) Act. This act was passed in 1970 by Congress. It ended up being a powerhouse of a tool to use against the Mafia crime families. The RICO Act enabled prosecutors to pursue the crime families and their sources of income, legal or illegal. The members of the Los Angeles crime family who were brought in under the RICO Act included the capos Mike Rizzitello, Luigi Gelfuso, and Jimmy Caci, as well as both Milano brothers. The information provided to law enforcement was primarily supplied by the Fiato brothers, who had become informants. The result of facing so many charges placed the family in a severely crippled state, with the organization nearly out of business. Rizzitello was acquitted of his original charges at his trial, only to be later convicted in 1989 for attempted murder. He was sentenced to 33 years in prison but would die in 2005 while serving his sentence. Both Milano brothers pleaded guilty to significantly lesser charges, resulting in Peter receiving a six-year sentence and Carmen a six-month sentence. However, neither ever admitted any connection to the Mafia. Nearly every member facing charges pleaded guilty to lesser charges to receive reduced sentences. The FBI believed it had won the war against the Los Angeles Mafia. When Peter Milano was in prison, Carmen Milano covered the role of acting boss for the family until his 1991 release.

Chief prosecutor James Henderson felt that "the guilty pleas, in which none of the defendants admitted any connection with the Mafia, 'absolutely crippled the family here'" (Gewertz, 1988). Luigi Gelfuso, Jr., Abraham Prins, John Mattia, and John Vaccaro refused to enter guilty pleas and instead opted for trials. Prins trial was placed on hold due to poor health.

Peter Milano pleaded guilty to a racketeering charge, while Carmen admitted to conspiring to extort money from loan shark customers who failed to pay their debts. The other family members entered pleas admitting to guilt in extortion conspiracies. One also pleaded guilty to cocaine distribution. Despite their light sentences, the prosecution saw the outcome as a significant victory. It saved the government the cost of a trial, and those who made pleas would likely return to their lives of crime upon release.

While the FBI firmly believed it had utterly decimated the ranks of the Los Angeles crime family, effectively ending its reign in the city, the Mafia would continue on to the present day. The Milano brothers continued running the family for several more years until Peter's death when a new boss would take over.

CHAPTER 7

THE FAMILY TODAY

The Los Angeles crime family once saw greatness as the ruler of the city. Under Jack Dragna, the members operated successful crime rackets, making an excellent income. They effortlessly muscled out contenders for their territories. Fast forward to the present Mafia, and things look quite a bit different. With severely diminished numbers and the majority of crime being committed by street gangs, not the Mafia, it is questionable whether they still exist or not. Severe damage would be caused yet again by members of the ranks, leading to the fall of the Los Angeles Mafia.

The Rise and Fall of the Los Angeles Mafia

A significant factor in the rise and fall of the Los Angeles Mafia was the testimony of the Fiato brothers. While the family thought they were recruiting two new solid members to the organization, they ended up bringing in future informants who would tell all their secrets. Throughout much of their time on the inside of the Los Angeles crime family, Anthony and Lawrence Fiato wore hidden wires and made recordings that were hand-delivered to the authorities. At the same time, the FBI was involved in capturing audio recordings from Peter Milano's home, his Rome Vending Co., and Luigi Gelfuso, Jr.'s home.

Many of the recordings obtained from 1984 to 1985 included conversations about collecting payments from local bookmakers and receiving tribute money from narcotics traffickers. Some discussions centered on the family making promises that they could deliver peace surrounding the labor on Hollywood productions.

While Peter Milano only served six years in prison for the charges that stemmed from the investigation the Fiato brothers assisted with, when he returned to take over the family once more, it was in a further weakened state. Since then, the Los Angeles crime family has advanced on Las Vegas alongside the Buffalo crime family. Carmen Milano made the move to Las Vegas in the early 1990s and the family placed him in charge of their interests in the city.

In 1998 Milano was one of several people named in a series of indictments that stemmed from a two-year investigation of organized crime in Southern Nevada. Milano admitted developing a fraudulent diamond scheme in the winter of 1996 with Herbert Blitzstein that was never carried out and laundering $50,000 from a food stamp fraud. (*Carmen Milano*, 2023)

Federal Judge Philip Martin Pro sentenced Carmen Milano to 21 months in prison in 2000. During the investigation, Milano directly violated the rules of omertà by revealing that he was the underboss of the Los Angeles Mafia. He also provided the information that Peter Milano was the boss. After disclosing this information, Carmen Milano considered entering witness protection but elected to serve his time in prison. Peter Milano didn't seek punishment for the omertà violation in a rare showing of Mafia mercy, allowing

Carmen to remain the underboss upon his return from incarceration on February 27, 2002. Carmen Milano died from cardiac arrest and renal failure on January 3, 2006.

During the Los Angeles crime family's expansion into Las Vegas, they received significant publicity relating to the murder of Herbert "Fat Herbie" Blitzstein. Tony "The Ant" Spilotro was sent by the Chicago Outfit out west to take control of their Las Vegas interests. To ensure his success, he brought several people associated with the Outfit as his muscle. One of these individuals was Herbert Blitzstein.

He was the son of a Jewish family in Chicago and was born on November 2, 1934. Blitzstein would later become involved in organized crime rackets in the late 1950s. He was well-known for his robust stature, standing 6 feet tall and weighing 300 pounds. Blitzstein made his earlier rise through the Chicago Outfit by using others as his stepping stones. He climbed up the ladder as certain individuals were taken out of their roles. He would eventually leave Chicago for Las Vegas following a gambling conviction. Once there, he operated Gold Rush, LTD with John Spilotro, Tony Spilotro's brother. The operation was said to be a jewelry store combined with an electronics factory. While running this business, Blitzstein gained significant expertise in the process of fencing stolen goods. Gold Rush, LTD opened in 1976, and Blitzstein hired a professional to install security to monitor the property and scanners to monitor police activity. It would become the go-to place for fencing stolen merchandise.

"Blitzstein was a monster of a man, and due to his ominous presence, Spilotro was rarely seen without him, although few in Las

Vegas would view him as being a brutal man" (May, 2009). Despite his stature, the impression Blitzstein gave was anything but what Spilotro wanted. Instead, many saw him as a stand-up kind of guy with a warm, outgoing personality—anything but the strong-arm type. "Blitzstein became a member of Spilotro's 'Hole in the Wall' gang. The gang was a burglary ring that operated with help from corrupt members of the Clark County Sheriff's Organized Crime Unit" (May, 2009). The FBI was able to capture the gang members while they were committing a robbery on July 4, 1981. Despite not being an active participant in the robbery, Blitzstein faced an indictment for racketeering charges. Just before this, he had spent several months in jail due to being in contempt of court. He was ordered to provide handwriting samples to the jury and refused to comply, as it would have implicated Spilotro.

The trial took place in 1986 but was declared a mistrial. One of the jurors had reported to the judge that they overheard two other members of the jury discussing bribes. Another trial was scheduled for mid-June, but Spilotro was murdered before it could start. In 1987, Blitzstein pleaded guilty to four different charges and received an eight-year sentence. While in prison, his health significantly deteriorated, with problems arising from diabetes and heart disease. He would have two bypass surgeries and several toes removed from his right foot before his release in 1991.

When he was released, he returned to a heavily changed Las Vegas. The newly enforced gaming laws and related government agency activity had significantly reduced Chicago Outfit's control over the city. Blitzstein, never a leader and always a follower, linked up with Ted Binion. At that time, Binion was currently suspended by the

Nevada State Gaming Commission. In December 1996, the State Gaming Control Board suggested adding Blitzstein's name to their Black Book of individuals considered disreputable. This move effectively banned him from the casinos.

In response, Blitzstein renewed his interest in the loan sharking industry. He also co-owned Any Auto Repair, an auto repair shop, with Joseph DeLuca. The shop was used as a front for running insurance fraud operations. Blitzstein's operations were raking in a good income by the mid-1990s. However, he lacked the protection he once had under Spilotro. The Los Angeles and Buffalo crime families had begun moving into the territory and were eyeing his interests. On January 6, 1977, DeLuca found Blitzstein dead in his home, the result of being shot three times in the head. The motive behind the murder was plain and simple greed to take over his illegal operations in Las Vegas. This was an interesting mob killing in that it was nothing more than a murder-for-hire plot. There was no one trying to become a made man on the other end of the trigger, which is typically the case in a mob-sanctioned hit.

It would later be uncovered that Joseph DeLuca, who had exceptional knowledge of Blitzstein's security system and home layout, orchestrated the murder and home burglary under the direction of Peter Vincent Caruso. The murder was approved by Buffalo and Los Angeles crime family members. It was alleged that Robert Panaro from the Buffalo family and Stephen Cino from the Los Angeles family were the ones to give the go-ahead on the murder. Five months after Blitzstein's murder, DeLuca came forward and revealed all the information he had regarding the murder in exchange for a significantly reduced sentence. Cino and

Panaro were the only involved people to go to trial but were found not guilty of his murder. Instead, they were charged with conspiracy to extort from him.

The Los Angeles Crime Family Today

By the 1990s, the Los Angeles crime family was estimated to have a severely diminished number of members, with approximately only 20 official family members. Since the Las Vegas indictments over Blitzstein's murder, the family has been in a higher state of seclusion without the rest of the world knowing their dealings. In fact, law enforcement has changed its tactics in dealing with organized crime to focus on gang activity among the Mexican and African American communities, as these groups are spread much wider and are far more prevalent than the Mafia is today in Los Angeles. When it comes to striking fear in the hearts of citizens, the Los Angeles Mafia is no longer one of the first groups that comes to mind.

It was believed that Peter Milano remained the boss until his passing on April 21, 2012. Despite this, it was also believed that his involvement in organized crime was significantly reduced from previous years, along with many members of the family. Some members, including Rocco Zangari and Russell Massetia, also moved out of state, leaving the family entirely. Other members, like Carmen Milano and Jimmy Caci, died from natural causes but had no natural successors to take their place in the ranks of the family. Unlike the East Coast, the Los Angeles area does not have a large Italian community for the family to recruit from. The family also faced significant issues with the rise of the local street gangs, battling for their interests in the various criminal rackets. While focusing on these street gangs, law enforcement considers the movement of East Coast Mafia families to the West Coast a cause for alarm.

It is assumed that Tommaso "Tommy" Gambino, son of Rosario Gambino, has been the acting boss of the Los Angeles Mafia since taking over in 2012. Rosario Gambino is a well-known member of the Gambino crime family who made headlines following the organization of a massive heroin cartel that he set up with his brothers in the 1970s and 1980s. He was born on January 12, 1942, in Palermo, Sicily. He and his two brothers became made men in the Sicilian Mafia. They are distant cousins of Gambino crime boss Carlo Gambino and his son Thomas Gambino. In 1962, their family moved to the United States, where Rosario would start his own family and have four children. The brothers would soon join the Gambino crime family. "Older brother Giovanni (who Americanized his name to John) was named a caporegime (captain) in the crime family, and Rosario and Giuseppe (who Americanized his name to Joseph) were his top lieutenants. Together the brothers formed a crew known as the 'Cherry Hill Gambinos,' named after their city of operation, Cherry Hill, New Jersey" (*Rosario Gambino*, 2023).

Rosario and Joseph partnered together to run a string of pizza shops called Father and Son Pizza. They ranged in location from Philadelphia to Camden to Delaware. While Rosario made a significant amount of money, he reported very little on his tax returns. His own lawyer could not tell anyone what his job was. The brothers were also linked to a series of arsons that occurred in the 1980s.

While the American Mafia was known to have established a drug trafficking ban, the Gambino crime family didn't stop smuggling in heroin. The Cherry Hill Gambinos were the ones who ultimately received the product as it came in from Sicily. An estimated $600 million was smuggled in annually. The profits from the sales were sent back to Sicily and invested in mostly legitimate businesses. In 1980, an arrest warrant was signed in Italy for Rosario Gambino and his brothers for their drug trafficking. The United States didn't provide extradition, so the trial proceeded without them, and they were found guilty. That same year, Rosario and Joseph were arrested for attempting to smuggle 91 pounds of heroin into the United States from Milan, Italy. However, they were both acquitted. In 1984, Gambino and several others were tried for narcotics trafficking. He was sentenced to 45 years in prison for the sale of heroin to an undercover officer.

Rosario Gambino made headlines again in 2001 when reports surfaced that in 1995 President Bill Clinton's half-brother Roger Clinton, Jr. had allegedly accepted $50,000 and a Rolex watch from Gambino's children. According to reports, in return, Roger said he could guarantee Anna and Tommaso, Rosario's children, a presidential pardon by President Clinton. (*Rosario Gambino*, 2023)

When the time came for the president to make his pardons before leaving office, Gambino's name was on the list to consider, but he chose not to pardon him.

During his time in prison, Rosario Gambino remained in close contact with Jimmy Caci and his son Tommaso of the Los Angeles crime family. The Italian government called for extradition in 2001 but was denied based on the court's determination that he had received similar charges in New York. After serving 22 years of his 45-year sentence, Gambino was released from prison in 2006 only to be transferred to a deportation center to be extradited to Italy. However, an immigration judge determined that he should not be deported due to the likelihood that he would be tortured for information regarding the Sicilian Mafia. Ultimately, he would be acquitted of drug trafficking charges on February 3, 2014. "In July 2019, Gambino was arrested in coordinated, international police raids triggered by a trans-Atlantic WhatsApp message" (*Rosario Gambino*, 2023).

Tommy Gambino is a Prosecco magnate in the Los Angeles area. Gambino Prosecco is an operation that he runs with his wife, Jules, who he met in 2001. The company was launched in 2015. While Gambino was born in New York in 1973, his family made a brief return to Palermo, Sicily, when he was a child. They finally settled in Los Angeles. "Having worked as an investment banker and property developer, Gambino decided to pursue his passion for wine by launching a Prosecco brand" (Shaw, 2021). With the couple's investment in the Prosecco business, they have plenty of opportunities to visit Italy throughout the year to check on the production of their goods.

Gambino allegedly inducted Musitano crime family associate Albert Iavarone into the family. It was reportedly done as a favor to the bosses in New York. Iavarone was selected as the intended individual to act as the liaison between the Canadian Mafia and the American Mafia. He was killed two weeks after this induction allegedly happened. The murder was reportedly ordered by the current boss of the Buffalo crime family, Joseph Todaro, Jr. The

Buffalo crime family had traditionally served as the liaison between the two Mafia groups, which resulted in the murder contract.

What once was a burgeoning crime family has been severely decimated over the years following the death of the "one true boss" of the city, Jack Dragna. It is unknown whether the Los Angeles crime family is still involved in criminal activities today. While it is assumed Gambino is the current boss, very little is known about the existing organization. The current underboss and consigliere are not public knowledge. Despite the Los Angeles crime family at one time being in control of the major rackets in the city, it is now likely just a shell of its former self. Tommy Gambino remains a man of mystery, with little information on how he entered the Mafia or came to be in the position of boss.

CONCLUSION

With its origins dating back to Sicily in the 19th century, the Mafia has always been a strong force to be reckoned with. Bringing together the Italian community in the world of organized crime, throughout history, we've seen the growth and spread of the American Mafia from the streets of New York City across the country. As Prohibition took hold nationwide, the Mafia seized its chance to become a powerhouse in the underworld. Key figures spread to strategic points around the country, establishing crime families, including in Los Angeles. Once Prohibition ended, their influence only expanded, taking on roles in other crime operations, such as gambling, pornography, and extortion.

While the Los Angeles crime family is now known as the Mickey Mouse Mafia, it was not always the case. Joseph Ardizzone was officially recognized as the first boss of the family, despite there being other leaders before him. He is credited with the formation of the official family, leading them toward what they would become under Jack Dragna. With his disappearance, the family only became stronger as his underboss took the reins. Under Dragna, the family had discipline and spread out across the criminal underworld of Los Angeles. The name Mickey Mouse Mafia came about with the bosses following him and since then has been incorrectly applied to the Dragna era. Many historians claim that Dragna was the only true crime boss the family had ever seen. Whether this is an accurate statement or not, it can be said that the family never saw greatness more so than when Dragna was the boss.

At the end of the Dragna era, Frank DeSimone took over, which in hindsight seems to have been a considerably poor choice of leadership for the family. DeSimone was never able to get the discipline or structure that the family had under Dragna, leaving them in a weakened state. With the increased crackdowns by law enforcement, he faced significant challenges that the two previous bosses didn't have to contend with. Because he feared the police, he had the family back off of their major money-making shakedowns, believing the victims would simply turn to the authorities for assistance. He would ultimately spend the rest of his time as boss in near seclusion because he found out about a plot to take him out. DeSimone would prove to be one of the weaker bosses of the Los Angeles crime family.

Nick Licata didn't prove to be much better of a leader than DeSimone. The family was largely in disarray throughout his reign. However, he managed to hold onto the title of boss. He was able to maintain good relations with the Detroit Mafia. Licata faced indictments and bad health throughout his time as boss. He would ultimately succumb to his health issues, leaving the family to Dominic Brooklier.

Running the family for a decade, Brooklier would spend most of that time in a jail cell. Despite that inconvenience, he was able to give direction and maintain his control while incarcerated. He was known for being involved with the murder of Frank Bompensiero, although he was never convicted. While he was in prison, several members of the family had the opportunity to run the organization, including Jimmy Fratianno and later, Peter Milano, who would become the next boss.

Peter Milano and his brother Carmen led the family for several years as boss and underboss, respectively. They came from a long line of Mafia family members, making it almost a natural progression for them to join a family. The Milano brothers were able to revamp the ailing family by inducting several new members. They also regained control over the gambling rackets, taking in the obligatory mob tax from every bookie in town. While their leadership started out strong, it would ultimately come to a crashing halt with the testimonies of the Fiato brothers—two men they believed would help improve the family's standing in the criminal underworld. With an arrest in 1984 and another in 1988, the family returned to its weakened state. Carmen also broke the oath of omertà but was forgiven by his brother in a rare show of mercy by a Mafia family.

It is believed that Peter Milano ran the family until his death in 2012 when he was replaced by Tommy Gambino. With minimal information about Gambino and his leadership, not much is known about the family today. More law enforcement focus is placed on eradicating the street gangs than on worrying about the Los Angeles crime family's activities.

With the family's steady decline since the 1956 death of Jack Dragna, the Chicago Outfit has represented them on The Commission. Throughout their long history, the Los Angeles crime family's numbers never exceeded those of the New York or Chicago families. Despite the Mafia having established the primary rule of omertà, most of the known information we have access to regarding the Los Angeles crime family comes from the testimony delivered by Jimmy Fratianno in the late 1970s. Since then, they have returned to shrouding themselves in mystery and keeping a low profile.

If you have enjoyed this book, please consider leaving a positive review so that like-minded readers may also find it. Your support means a lot and will help others find their way to the material they enjoy.

REFERENCES

About the California based Los Angeles Mafia family. (2016, January 15). American Mafia. https://www.americanmafia.org/families/about-the-california-based-los-angeles-mafia-family/

Alexander, K. (2022.). *La Cosa Nostra – American Mafia.* Legends of America. https://www.legendsofamerica.com/la-cosa-nostra/

Alleged L.A. Mafia chief goes to jail. (1969, July 10). *The Spokesman-Review.* https://news.google.com/newspapers?id=QCUSAAAAIBAJ&sjid=WOwDAAAAIBAJ&pg=2155

America's Untold Stories. (n.d.). *Mickey Cohen and the Battle of the Sunset Strip.* YouTube. https://www.youtube.com/live/0iWzVFFFTA4?feature=share

Banning, D. (2019, June 12). *Los Angeles mobster's gambling ring.* Gambling History. https://gambling-history.com/los-angeles-mobsters-gambling-ring/

Benigno, F. (2018). *Rethinking the origins of the Sicilian Mafia: A new interpretation.* Crime, Histoire & Sociétés, 22(1), 107–130. https://doi.org/10.4000/chs.2143

Black Hand | American criminal organization. (n.d.). Encyclopedia Britannica. https://www.britannica.com/topic/Black-Hand-American-criminal-organization

Bloodletters & Badmen. (n.d.). *Mobster - Jack Dragna & the Mickey Mouse Mafia.* YouTube. https://youtu.be/WVJURPtyggg

Bootlegging | definition, history, & facts. (2017, June 23). Encyclopedia Britannica. https://www.britannica.com/topic/bootlegging

Bugsy Siegel | biography, crimes, & facts. (n.d.). Encyclopedia Britannica. https://www.britannica.com/biography/Bugsy-Siegel

Capeci, J. (2002). *The complete idiot's guide to the Mafia.* In *Internet Archive.* https://archive.org/details/completeidiotsgu0000cape/page/n8/mode/1up

Carmen Milano. (2023, July 27). In *Wikipedia.* https://en.wikipedia.org/wiki/Carmen_Milano

Cleveland crime family. (2023, February 22). In Wikipedia. https://en.wikipedia.org/wiki/Cleveland_crime_family

Cohen, J. (1970, July 25). San Bernardino officials once vouched for L.A. Mafia figure. The Los Angeles Times. https://www.newspapers.com/image/386208078/?terms=%22San%20Bernardino%20Officials%20Once%20Vouched%22&match=1

D.P. Brooklier, 70; a jailed mobster. (1984, July 22). The New York Times. https://www.nytimes.com/1984/07/22/obituaries/dp-brooklier-70-a-jailed-mobster.html

Danieljbmitchell. (n.d.). *Organized crime in Los Angeles in 1930s*. YouTube. https://youtu.be/UOv5PWKPUh8

Death of a psychopath: How mob boss who killed men for the kick finally met his match. (n.d.). Free Online Library. https://www.thefreelibrary.com/Death+of+a+psychopath%3A+How+mob+boss+who+killed+men+for+the+kick...-a0564731406

Definition of Mafia. (n.d.). Merriam-Webster. https://www.merriam-webster.com/dictionary/Mafia

Definition of wise guy. (2023, July 8). Merriam-Webster. https://www.merriam-webster.com/dictionary/wise%20guy

Dominic Brooklier. (2022, November 2). In *Wikipedia*. https://en.wikipedia.org/wiki/Dominic_Brooklier

Dragna rule seen in bookie racket. (1953, May 11). *The Los Angeles Times*, 2. https://www.newspapers.com/article/the-los-angeles-times/30797989/

Dragna to fight deportation. (1953, March 3). *Sarasota Herald-Tribune*. https://news.google.com/newspapers?id=RHEjAAAAIBAJ&dq=jack%20dragna&pg=5204%2C648774

Dunn, M. (2022, March 9). W*hy the Mafia lived and died by the code of silence known as omertà*. All That's Interesting. https://allthatsinteresting.com/omerta

Frank Bompensiero. (2023, May 29). In *Wikipedia*. https://en.wikipedia.org/wiki/Frank_Bompensiero

Frank DeSimone. (2023, June 7). In *Wikipedia*. https://en.wikipedia.org/wiki/Frank_DeSimone

Gewertz, C. (1988, March 29). *The reputed boss and under-boss of the Southern California...* UPI Archives. https://www.upi.com/Archives/1988/03/29/The-reputed-boss-and-under-boss-of-the-Southern-California/9076575614800/

Graham, J. H. (2020, December 5). *The Sunset Strip.* J. H. Graham. https://jhgraham.com/category/the-sunset-strip/

Graham, J. H. (2022, May 26). *Jack Dragna.* J. H. Graham. https://jhgraham.com/tag/jack-dragna/

Hazlitt, B. (1974, October 21). Nick Licata Dies; headed L.A. area Mafia for 6 years. *The Los Angeles Times.* https://www.newspapers.com/image/386005035/?terms=%22Nick%20Licata%22&match=1

Herbert Blitzstein. (2023, August 12). In *Wikipedia.* https://en.wikipedia.org/wiki/Herbert_Blitzstein

History. (2019, February 21). *How prohibition created the Mafia.* YouTube. https://youtu.be/N-K60XXaPKw

History.com Editors. (2009, November 9). *Bugsy Siegel.* History. https://www.history.com/topics/crime/bugsy-siegel

History.com Editors. (2018a, August 21). *Crime in the Great Depression.* History. https://www.history.com/topics/great-depression/crime-in-the-great-depression#section_1

History.com Editors. (2018b, August 21). *Mafia in the United States.* History. https://www.history.com/topics/crime/mafia-in-the-united-states

History.com Editors. (2019, February 22). *Origins of the Mafia*. *History*. https://www.history.com/topics/crime/origins-of-the-mafia

How is a Mafia family structured? (n.d.). National Crime Syndicate. https://www.nationalcrimesyndicate.com/mafia-family-structured/

Hunt, T. (n.d.-a). *Brooklier, Dominic (1914-1984)*. The American Mafia—Who Was Who. Retrieved August 6, 2023, from http://mob-who.blogspot.com/2011/04/brooklier-dominic-1914-1984.html

Hunt, T. (n.d.-b). *DeSimone, Frank (1909-1967)*. The American Mafia—Who Was Who. Retrieved August 6, 2023, from http://mob-who.blogspot.com/2011/04/desimone-frank-1909-1967.html

Hunt, T. (n.d.-c). *Licata, Nicola "Nick" (1897-1974)*. The American Mafia—Who Was Who. http://mob-who.blogspot.com/2011/05/licata-nicola-nick-1897-1974.html

Hunt, T. (2019, October 15). *Wealthy Los Angeles-area Mafia leader vanishes*. The Writers of Wrongs. http://www.writersofwrongs.com/2019/10/wealthy-los-angeles-area-mafia-leader.html

Jack Dragna. (2023, June 12). In *Wikipedia*. https://en.wikipedia.org/wiki/Jack_Dragna

Jack Dragna eludes arrest in the wake of the failed attempt on Mickey Cohen. (1950, February 15). The Los Angeles Times, 1. https://www.newspapers.com/article/the-los-angeles-times-jack-dragna-eludes/37264401/

Jimmy Fratianno. (2023, July 31). In *Wikipedia*. https://en.wikipedia.org/wiki/Jimmy_Fratianno

Joseph Dippolito. (2023, March 4). In *Wikipedia*. https://en.wikipedia.org/wiki/Joseph_Dippolito

Knox, M. (2020, May 18). *5 L.A. mob murders*. Medium. https://mikeknoxcomedy.medium.com/5-l-a-mob-murders-e02ccefe3b26

Loan shark. (2019, November 5). Wikipedia; Wikimedia Foundation. https://en.wikipedia.org/wiki/Loan_shark

Los Angeles crime family. (n.d.). Liquisearch. https://www.liquisearch.com/los_angeles_crime_family

Los Angeles crime family. (2023, August 2). In *Wikipedia*. https://en.wikipedia.org/wiki/Los_Angeles_crime_family

Los Angeles crime family - history. (n.d.). Liquisearch. https://www.liquisearch.com/los_angeles_crime_family/history

Los Angeles crime family - origins and predecessors. (n.d.). Liquisearch. https://www.liquisearch.com/los_angeles_crime_family/origins_and_predecessors

Los Angeles crime family bosses. (n.d.). American Mafia History. https://mafiahistory.us/maf-b-la.html

Mafia | organized crime. (2019). Encyclopedia Britannica. https://www.britannica.com/topic/Mafia

Mafia org chart. (2016). Federal Bureau of Investigation. https://www.fbi.gov/file-repository/mafia-family-tree.pdf/view

May, A. (2009, October 14). *Greed in the desert: The murder of Herbert Blitzstein.* Crime Magazine. http://www.crimemagazine.com/greed-desert-murder-herbert-blitzstein

Meares, H. (2019, February 14). *When mobsters and movie stars ruled the Sunset Strip.* Curbed LA. https://la.curbed.com/2019/2/14/18215017/sunset-strip-los-angeles-history-mickey-cohen

Mickey Cohen. (n.d.). Crime Museum. https://www.crimemuseum.org/crime-library/organized-crime/mickey-cohen/

Mob leader makes getaway in California. (1950, February 15). *Tampa Bay Times,* 3. https://www.newspapers.com/article/tampa-bay-times/129519777/

The Mob Museum. (2022). *Prohibition profits transformed the mob.* Prohibition. https://prohibition.themobmuseum.org/the-history/the-rise-of-organized-crime/the-mob-during-prohibition/

Mobster gone; police fear for his safety. (1950, February 15). *Sarasota Herald-Tribune.* https://news.google.com/newspapers?id=I-IcAAAAIBAJ&dq=tom-dragna&pg=3778%2C4274974

Momo Adamo. (2023, May 15). In *Wikipedia.* https://en.wikipedia.org/wiki/Momo_Adamo

Morrison, P. (2021, June 1). Why was the mob in L.A. so much quieter than in Chicago or New York? *Los Angeles Times.* https://www.latimes.com/california/story/2021-06-01/why-was-the-mob-in-l-a-so-much-quieter-than-chicago-or-new-york

Murphy, K. (1987, June 29). The L.A. mob: Eking out a living working the streets. The *Los Angeles Times*, 5. https://www.newspapers.com/article/the-los-angeles-times-milano-mob-1/82865618/

Murphy, K. (1988a, March 30). 7 alleged Southland Mafia figures enter guilty pleas. *The Los Angeles Times*. https://www.newspapers.com/image/404200846/?terms=7%20Alleged%20Southland%20mafia&match=1

Murphy, K. (1988b, March 30). The rise and fall of L.A.'s "Mickey Mouse Mafia." *The Lost Angeles Times*. https://www.newspapers.com/image/404203542/?terms=rise%20and%20fall%20of%20mickey%20mouse%20mafia

Nick Licata (mobster). (2023, March 4). In *Wikipedia*. https://en.wikipedia.org/wiki/Nick_Licata_(mobster)

Nick Licata released on $2,500 bond. (1970, May 5). *Los Angeles Evening Citizen News*. https://www.newspapers.com/image/684750555/?terms=%22Nick%20Licata%22&match=1

Niotta, J. M. (n.d.). *Dragna*. JMichaelniottaphd. https://www.jmichaelniotta.com/jack-dragna

Niotta, J. M. (2018a, March 5). *Peacekeepers and killers: The early days of Los Angeles*. National Crime Syndicate. https://www.nationalcrimesyndicate.com/peacekeepers-killers-installment-one-early-days-los-angeles/

Niotta, J. M. (2018b, October 23). *Jack Dragna biography: The early days of Los Angeles with Dr. J. Michael Niotta*. National

Crime Syndicate. https://www.nationalcrimesyndicate.com/jack-dragna-biography-the-early-days-of-los-angeles/

Organized crime loses its foothold. (2002, July 2). *Las Vegas Sun Newspaper.* https://lasvegassun.com/news/2002/jul/02/organized-crime-loses-its-foothold/

Pearson, D. (1962, February 9). Thriller films pale in comparison with California files on crime. *Tampa Bay Times.* https://www.newspapers.com/image/318073302/?terms=de%20Simone&match=1

Peter Milano. (2023, July 31). In *Wikipedia.* https://en.wikipedia.org/wiki/Peter_Milano

Picand, Y., & Dutoit, D. (n.d.). *Los Angeles crime family : Definition of Los Angeles crime family and synonyms of Los Angeles crime family.* SensAgent. https://dictionary.sensagent.com/Los%20Angeles%20crime%20family/en-en/#Dragna_era

Prohibition and organised crime. (2015, September 3). RGS History. https://rgshistory.com/prohibition-and-organised-crime/

Racket. (2022, June 8). Cambridge Dictionary. https://dictionary.cambridge.org/us/dictionary/english/racket

Radzicki McManus, M., & Phipps, M. (2015, February 27). *10 businesses supposedly controlled by the Mafia.* HowStuffWorks. https://people.howstuffworks.com/10-businesses-supposedly-controlled-by-the-mafia.htm

Robb, B. J. (2014). *A brief history of gangsters.* In Google Books. Little, Brown Book Group.

https://books.google.com/books?id=25RIDwAAQBAJ&pg=PT99&lpg=PT99&dq=joe+ardizzone+la+mafia&source=bl&ots=xZBHV_0_bP&sig=ACfU3U0pewzIX4QVce8eCrHLslDU2zhX8g&hl=en&sa=X&ved=2ahUKEwjhkuGZ0cCAAxW7bzABHUwHBRI4RhDoAXoECAIQAw#v=onepage&q=joe%20ardizzone%20la%20mafia&f=false

Roos, D. (2019, January 14). *How Prohibition put the "organized" in organized crime*. History. https://www.history.com/news/prohibition-organized-crime-al-capone

Rosario Gambino. (2023, June 24). In *Wikipedia*. https://en.wikipedia.org/wiki/Rosario_Gambino

Server, L. (2018, December 7). *How psychotic mob boss who killed men for the kick finally met his match*. Mirror. https://www.mirror.co.uk/news/real-life-stories/death-psychopath-how-mob-boss-13696839

Shaw, L. (2021, June 14). The big interview: Tommy and Jules Gambino. The Drinks Business. https://www.thedrinksbusiness.com/2021/06/the-big-interview-tommy-and-jules-gambino/

Siegel slaying still mystery. (1947, June 24). Nevada State Journal, 10. https://www.newspapers.com/article/nevada-state-journal-siegel-slaying-stil/30129739/

Sifakis, C. (2010). The Mafia encyclopedia. In Internet Archive. Facts on File Inc, /DBA Infobase Publishing. https://archive.org/details/mafiaencyclopedi00sifa_0/page/62/mode/1up?q=brooklier

Sullivan, N. (2014). *American organized crime of the 1920s*. Study. https://study.com/academy/lesson/american-organized-crime-of-the-1920s.html

Tom Dragna death Oct 2 1977. (1977, October 2). *Valley News, 36*. https://www.newspapers.com/article/32938920/tom-dragna-death-oct-2-1977/

Tuohy, J. W. (2023). *Bugsy*. American Mafia. http://www.americanmafia.com/Feature_Articles_166.html

Williamdefalco. (n.d.). Mafia & gangsters: Joseph "Joe Iron Man" Ardizzone, Los Angeles crime family chief who disappeared. YouTube. https://youtu.be/3jZXHOqC1HI

Younger, E. J. (1978). Organized crime control commission first report II. https://www.ojp.gov/pdffiles1/Digitization/79411NCJRS.pdf

www.ingramcontent.com/pod-product-compliance
Lightning Source LLC
Chambersburg PA
CBHW071402080526
44587CB00017B/3156